DOROTHY

Neil Rathmell was born in 1947 and grew up in Yorkshire. He read English at Jesus College, Cambridge. His first novel, *The Old School*, was published by Faber & Faber in 1976. His short fiction has been published in literary magazines including *Ambit*, *Prole*, *Popshot* and *The Penny Dreadful*. His plays have been produced by youth theatres and amateur drama groups in the UK, India and the Czech Republic. After a career in education which took him to Cheshire, County Durham and Shropshire, he is now back in Yorkshire enjoying retirement with his wife, Jaspreet.

Dorothy

Neil Rathmell

Valley Press

First published in 2023 by Valley Press
Woodend, The Crescent, Scarborough, YO11 2PW
www.valleypressuk.com

First edition, first printing (May 2023)

ISBN 978-1-915606-32-7
Cat. no. VP0221

Text and cover design by Jamie McGarry.
Cover photograph by Caroline Ingram.

Printed and bound in Great Britain by
Imprint Digital, Upton Pyne, Exeter.

Contents

To my daughters

Our Dot

this one's different
Jack said when he saw the baby

she was the runt of the litter
John William had come first
Dinah came seven years later
both sturdy infants
now this one
it seemed to happen every seven years
whether they liked it or not

but that wasn't what he meant
Annie didn't know what he meant
but she knew it wasn't that

growing up in a harbour town
before she knew him
he used to dive for pennies in the harbour

when he was old enough to leave home
he left
taking nothing with him
because they gave him nothing to take

he was small but fearless
fierce like a dog
he earned money from bare-knuckle boxing

but when he married Annie
a bonny girl
not much more than half his age
he promised to give it up

one of his eyes was half closed
but that happened later
when a cow kicked him

their first house was a tied cottage
at the top of a hill
Annie put chairs outside
where people could sit and get their breath back
she sold them home-made lemonade
a penny a glass

she learned to milk
they worked on farms
and saved until they had enough
to pay the rent
on a little farm of their own

when he came home one night
with his face cut and bruised
she thought he had broken his promise
and gone boxing again
but she was wrong
he had taken a drunken chap home to his wife
and when she came to the door
she threw a teapot at him

when the baby didn't thrive
Jack sent for the doctor
who took one look at her

sat down at the kitchen table
and said she was dying

Jack threw him out
they fed the baby
on bread soaked in bacon fat
and she began to thrive

2.

the house was full of people
but hardly anyone spoke
everyone was sad
Dorothy didn't know why

a lady picked her up
and carried her upstairs

there he is
she said
you won't see your daddy again
he's gone now

Dorothy thought she must be wrong
because she could see him
lying on the bed
with his eyes closed

take your last look at him
and try to remember
the lady said
then she put her down
and told her to go out and play

3

John William looked older than he was
people waved white feathers at him
jeered and called him a coward
for not joining up
to fight for King and Country

there was no point in arguing
nobody believed him
all he could do was ignore them

Jack would have fought if he could
but he was getting on and anyway
farming was a reserved occupation

when the war was over he fell ill
he told Annie he was dying
she said
you're not dying Jack
nay lass
he said
I've never lied to you before
and I'm not going to start now

he died of pneumonia
brought on by the Spanish flu
but before he died
he told her to look after the little one
knowing that the other two
could take care of themselves

there was an outbreak of foot and mouth then
it never rains but it pours
Annie said

when that was over
she had to give up the farm
John William said he could run it
Cedric and the others thought different
we'll work for you missis
they said
but not for him
he's too big for his boots

Annie gave up the tenancy
sold off the stock
and took a shop in Leeds

instead of selling lemonade at a penny a glass
to people toiling up a hill
she sold beer and groceries
to people toiling in factories

she and her children lived over the shop
she would be able to give it up
when she had enough put by
to live off the interest

the shop had running water
instead of a pump
every day Dinah and John William
turned the tap
on and off
on and off
on and off

Dorothy had never had to pump water
the mystery of the tap
meant nothing to the little one

she missed her daddy
missed the farm
the fields
the trees
the sunlight
the mist
the hedgerows
the flowers
the birds
the cows

hated the shop
the streets
the houses
the pavements
the street lamps
the fog
the people
the noise

she wanted to know
why they had brought her here
but none of them would tell her
not our Dinah
not our John Willy
not our mam

it wasn't fair

4.

there were weeds growing
in the pavement outside the shop
Dorothy filled a cup with water from the tap
and went out to water them

have you seen our Dot?
Dinah said to Annie
she's watering the weeds!

there was nobody in the shop
so they went out to look

Edith Glover joined them
shopping basket on her arm
jug in hand
wanting to know what was going on

it's our Dot
Annie said
she's doing a spot of gardening

Dinah said
she's daft isn't she

Edith laughed and said
bless her!

the two women went into the shop
Annie filled Edith's jug with a quart of ale
Dinah stayed to watch her sister

amused by her methodical watering
of the weeds on the pavement
each dandelion tuft
each blade of grass
each dusty leaf
getting its fair share of the water
one drop at a time

5.

John Willy moved out

if he couldn't run the farm
he wanted to run something else

there was a bottom rung on every ladder

the first ladder that he chose
was the brewery
he got a job as
assistant drayman

the brewery gave all its workers
free beer at the end of their shift
Annie got that stopped
which made her popular
with the wives and mothers
unpopular with the workers
and not unpopular with the brewery
which saved money by it

the second ladder that John Willy chose

or that by luck or chance or fate
chose him
was the ladder of coal
everyone needed coal
John Willy saw an opportunity
caught hold of the bottom rung
and became a coal man

dangling his legs off the back of the cart
he jumps off when they stop
heaves a hundredweight sack of coal
onto his broad back
tips it into somebody's coal house
down somebody's coal chute
knocks on somebody's door
takes the half-crown
or the ten-bob note
that the housewife holds out

the man with his name
on the side of the cart
gees up the horse
hearing the horse's hooves
clip-clopping past him
on the cobbles
John Willy jumps back on

his legs dangling
he looks back at the housewife
if she's still there
which she often is
favouring her with a wink
if she favours him with a wave
which she often does

when John Willy comes home for his dinner
and stays to play with her
Dorothy feels a bubbling inside
like water boiling in the copper on washing day
or the lid of the kettle rattling at teatime

when he says
come here our Dot!
and chases her
with his big coal-black hands
Annie says
don't you dare
that frock's clean on

when he puts a black smudge
on her nose
Annie says
wash that off now
Dinah says
leave it to me
Dorothy says
ow! you're hurting me!
Dinah rubs harder

on his way out
John Willy says
leave her alone

6.

Mary was a millhand
she wasn't our Mary
she was just Mary
she helped Annie in the shop
in down times
when the hands were laid off

she was older than Dinah
but not by much
she was young and pretty
Dorothy thought so anyway

she would have been happy
staying at home with Mary
but she had to go to school

she could have gone to the school
where the poor children went
the bare-bottom children
who sat on the steps
and played in the street
but Annie
mindful of Jack's instructions
paid for her to go to a school
run by two unmarried sisters

that was where it was realised
that Dorothy was short-sighted
the sisters made her sit at the front
and gave her a note to take home
saying she needed to have her eyes tested

the glasses Annie got for her
had thick lenses
that made the glasses so heavy
they were always sliding down her nose
and she was always pushing them up again

Dinah made fun of her
teased her
mimicked her
until she lost her temper
and burst into tears

Annie thought the little one
should learn to stick up for herself

the girls at school were nice
so were the bare-bottom children
who played in the street
but Annie didn't let her play with them
if she did and Dinah saw her
she would tell on her
she would say
our Dot's been playing with them mucky kids again
then she would go back out and say
our mam says you have to come in

Dorothy's best friend at school
was Sarah Deichmann
who was Jewish
there were a lot of Jews where they lived

so many that Dorothy once said
and Dinah often repeated
Mummy am I a Jew?

laying fires on Friday night
in the hearths of Jewish families
was a source of income for the mothers
of the bare-bottom children
that Dorothy used to play with
before she knew any better

Sarah invited Dorothy to her birthday party
Annie bought her a new dress
the next time Mary came
she wanted to hear all about it
Dorothy told her about Sarah's big house
and the games they played
and the garden where they ran about
and the food that Sarah's mother made

you must invite her to your party
Mary said
I'd like to meet her

Dorothy nodded
but she knew she could never do that
she would be too ashamed
Sarah lived in a nice house with a garden
Dorothy lived over a shop in a street
where bare-bottom children played

7.

Dorothy's godmother lived in an almshouse
they went to see her sometimes
she was dressed all in black
from bonnet to boots
the room was dark
and cold

Dorothy would have held her mother's hand
if it had been permitted
but it was not
Annie did not approve
of public displays of affection
nor did she approve
of private displays of affection

Dorothy sat on a chair
pushing her glasses up
feeling cold
and afraid of the dark
her mother and godmother talked
she heard their voices
but not what they were saying

when they left
her godmother gave her a penny
which she spent on a penn'orth of peas
at the market

Dinah made fun of her
why don't you buy sweets like everybody else?
you're not normal

Dorothy liked podding the peas
eating them one by one
from the pod
she didn't care what Dinah said

better than the penny her godmother gave her
were the books Aunt Sar'ann brought
when she came to call

the first was *Daddy Long Legs*
it was the first book she ever read
as soon as she finished it
she read it again
and kept on reading it
until Aunt Sar'ann brought her another one

books were like pea pods with people inside
better because when she opened the book again
the people were still there
the story was still there
just as she remembered it
a different world
just for her

she was safe there
between the covers
inside the pod with the peas

8.

John Willy caught the next rung
sooner than might have been expected
except by those who knew him

he had the doggedness of his father
and the enterprise of his mother

seeing his chance
when the man with his name
on the side of the cart
dropped dead with the reins in his hands
John Willy took them from him
borrowed enough money from Annie
to buy the horse and cart
from the man's widow
and went on serving the same customers
on the same round
without missing a delivery

his transition to self-employed manhood
was complete when he fell in love
with a girl called Milly
and married her

Dinah and Dorothy were bridesmaids
Annie bought the material for their dresses
Dinah made them

I'll make yours long
she said to Dorothy
so your fat knees won't show

Milly said both her bridesmaids looked lovely

9.

do you want to come and stay with us for a few days?
Mary said

Mam won't let me
Dorothy said

yes she will
said Mary
I've asked her

Dorothy began to shake
what's the matter?
am I really going?
of course you are!
Dorothy shook so much
she was like a jug full of water
splashing tears everywhere
Mary put her arms around her
oh you are a love!
she said

the house where Mary lived
with her mam and dad and two young brothers
was halfway up a steep hill
if the houses hadn't been joined together
they looked as if they would have slid down
and landed in a heap at the bottom

the first time they caught the bus to Mary's house
she held Mary's hand all the way
they got there at teatime
Mary's family were all there
they sat round a table to have tea
which was ham sandwiches

Dorothy was too shy to talk
you tell them
she said to Mary
whenever she was asked a question

nobody seemed to mind

she stayed for two days
sleeping with Mary
never leaving her side
day or night

Mary took her to see her best friend
who had been to school with her
and worked with her at the mill
but Dorothy never said a word

she cried when they went back on the bus
and said it had been the best time
she had ever had
in her whole life
and please could she go again

of course you can
Mary said
but only if you promise to talk

the next time they went
when she was safely off the bus
walking up the hill
holding Mary's hand
she said
I won't talk Mary

10.

Annie's savings were mounting nicely
but the interest was not yet enough to live on
she would have to wait another three years
at least

then she had an idea

she calculated that if she made the attic
into another bedroom
she could take in a lodger
the rent would be a good return
on her investment
and let her give up the shop
sooner than she had planned

she could not however
have foreseen
what the joiner found
in the attic

worse than a skeleton in a cupboard
is the skeleton of a baby in the attic

a rumour quickly went round
that it was Dinah's

she had put on weight
hadn't she?
they had thought it was puppy fat
but really

at the inquest
the coroner returned an open verdict

the joiner finished his work
Annie advertised for a lodger
Dinah found work further off
and moved into lodgings

the rumours died down
despite the best efforts of some
to keep them alive
but as is the way with rumours
they never quite went away

II.

there was a piano in the back room
which nobody had ever played
until the lodger moved in
he could not read music
but he knew how to vamp
he called it playing by ear
he could play anything you asked for

Dorothy had heard nothing like it before
except the barrel organ
played by the ting-a-lairy man
who passed sometimes down the street

his name was Arthur
Arthur she would say
when he came in from work
please will you play something?
and knelt on the couch to listen

Annie was not so easily taken in
she thought he was a show-off
a hail-fellow-well-met type
but he cheered the place up in his way
and after recent events
the place needed cheering up

he made up to Mary when she was there
but that didn't trouble her
Mary was old enough to look after herself
and Arthur was old enough to be her father
it was all in fun

until she found Dot sitting on his knee
while he played the piano with one hand
and put the other one where it shouldn't be

out!
she said
out now!

when Dorothy asked why she had sent him away
she said he had fallen behind with his rent

she also took the opportunity to tell her
never to let anyone touch her
there

I 2.

when Jack and Milly were married
(he was Jack now
like his father
JW on the side of the cart)
they rented a little cottage of their own

Annie and Dorothy went to see them
walking out of the city
leaving the houses behind
until they were out in the country
and came to the cottage

Dorothy pointed to a wooden sign
on the wall
JACMIL
what does that mean?

it's a bit of daftness
Annie said
he's put their names together
to make a name for the house

Jack was out on his rounds
Milly had baked a cake
they could smell it when they went in
she made a pot of tea
and sat them down at the kitchen table

well Dot
Milly said
are you enjoying your summer holidays?
Dorothy looked at her mother
Annie said
she helps me round the house
when she hasn't got her nose in a book
Milly said
do you like reading?
Dorothy looked at her mother
Annie said
it's all she ever does
Milly said
I've got some books you might like
she pointed to a bookcase under the window
go and have a look
Dorothy looked at her mother
Annie said
what do you say?
Dorothy said
please may I leave the table?
Annie said
don't ask me
ask your sister-in-law
Milly said
there's no need to stand on ceremony
off you go

Dorothy looked at her mother
Milly gave Dorothy a push
go on
she said
see if you can find one you like

Dorothy sat on the floor
in front of the wooden bookcase
which Milly told Annie
Jack had made for her
but only after a lot of nagging

aye well
Annie said
you mun start as you mean to go on

Dorothy chose a book
with a title she liked
saying it to herself soundlessly
she went back to the table
and stood as if in an invisible queue
waiting to be served

go on then
Annie said
ask!
Milly held out her hand for the book
let's see
oh aye!
she said
giving it back
Wuthering Heights
you'll like that

Dorothy ran back
to her place on the floor
opened the book
and started to read

she was still reading when Jack came home
hello our Dot
he said
Dorothy didn't hear
Annie said
you're not going deaf as well are you?
your brother's talking to you!
Jack said
leave her alone
she's all right

when it was time to go
Dorothy closed the book
and put it back on the bookshelf
Milly said
aren't you going to take it with you?
you can if you want
Dorothy looked at her mother
Annie said
ask Milly
it's not my book
it's hers
Dorothy looked at the floor
please may I borrow it?
she said
Jack said
you're a funny little thing aren't you?

13.

heavy rain in February caused the river
that ran through the city
to break its banks

the shop was on higher ground
but Annie moved all her stock off the floor
just in case
especially the dry goods
stored in sacks
flour salt sugar

water came up out of the drains into the street
it came up in the cellar too

Dorothy stood at the top of the steps
with her hand on the wall
looking down into the dark
where barrels were floating
on water so black and shiny
it looked like tarpaulin
she felt as if things were coming loose
from their moorings
as if anything could happen
as if she might be next

Annie insisted on good behaviour in the shop
her customers rarely disobeyed
any who did were barred

outside in the street
they were a law unto themselves
unless the police were involved
which sometimes happened
but not often
mostly it was domestic disputes
drunk and disorderly
neighbours falling out
Annie never took sides
not in here
she said
keep it to yourself
I don't want to know
I won't tell you again
and I won't have any bad language
her customers knew better than to argue

she never joined in with gossip
but she was never in any doubt
who was in the right
and when rumours went round
she always knew who was behind them
and whether there was any truth in it

so when Mrs Gawthorpe
took Mrs Outhwaite to court for slander

and Mrs Outhwaite was found guilty
and fined ten shillings plus costs
Annie knew who was really to blame
so when Mrs Outhwaite asked the judge
if she could be fined for thinking it
because she still thought it
Annie was glad she'd got the last word

15.

Francis Leeming LLB
Frank to his friends
Mr Leeming to Annie
had known her late husband
as a tenant farmer
who rented his farm
from one of his clients

shocked and saddened by his death
as much as his client had been
by the loss of a good tenant
if not more so
Mr Leeming went on to occupy a place
in Annie's affairs somewhere between
an unpaid family solicitor
and a family friend

where money and the law were concerned
she always turned to him
if not for advice
for reassurance

you don't need me to advise you
he said
you're prudent enough as it is
you're not one to take risks

when John Willy needed money to buy the cart
she gave it to him as a loan
and made him sign for it
John Willy said she was mean and hard-hearted
but she would not be moved

about the skeleton in the attic
Mr Leeming advised her only to tell the truth
take no notice of the rumours
he said
there will always be rumours
he did not doubt
that Annie had told the truth
only that the truth
might not have been
what she thought it was

she kept the shop for another year
after Dinah had gone
by which time
the interest on her savings
was enough for them to live on
just her and the little one
and with Mr Leeming's approval
she gave up the tenancy on the shop
and rented a house instead

The village

the best way to get to know a place
Annie said
was to walk

the best time to walk
she said
was in the evening

so every evening
after tea
they went out for a walk

the village
to those who lived there
was just the village

when people went out
they went
down the village

walking around the village
with her mother
after tea

seeing hedgerows
instead of houses
hearing birds sing

watching the wind
make waves
in the fields

Dorothy learned the village names
Brook Foot
Throstle Nest

Scotland Lane
Roman Road
Bluebell Woods

Crag Woods
Old Mill Beck
Town Street

Town Street was where
the shops were
all kinds of shops

grocers
greengrocers
butchers

newsagents
barbers
hairdressers

a shoe shop
a dress shop
a toy shop

a bank
a post office
a police station

a chemist
a library
public houses

black bull
brown cow
grey mare

from top to bottom
no shop to remind her
of the one they had left behind

with barrels in the cellar
and bare-bottom children
in the street

2.

the parish church at the top of the hill
had a spire you could see
for miles around

there were chapels too
which they passed every day
on their evening walk

two on Town Street
Primitives at the top
Wesleyans at the bottom

the top of Town Street
was closer to home
so Annie chose the Prims

they went to chapel
morning and evening
every Sunday

on Sunday afternoons
Annie took the little one
to Sunday school

on weekdays she took her
to the school in the village
where the other children went

until she found a school
she could afford to pay for
and sent her there instead

Dorothy went to school on the tram
making friends with girls
who lived somewhere else

her friends were friends at school
at home instead of playing out
she stayed in with her mother

3.

I don't like going on the tram
I don't like that school
I want to go to the school in the village
like everybody else

I'm doing what your father would have wanted
let that be an end to it

4.

Wuthering Heights
Black Beauty
A Christmas Carol

The Mill on the Floss
David Copperfield
(twice)

Jane Eyre
Silas Marner
Heidi

between the covers
inside the pod
with the peas

Dorothy's books
grew in
different gardens

some she picked
in the bookcase
at Jacmil

Aunt Sar'ann
picked some for her
in her secret garden

some she found growing wild
at the public library
in Town Street

please can we stop at the library
I've got to return my book
or I'll have to pay a fine

Annie went on
down Town Street
to finish her shopping

mind you're waiting outside
when I get back
she said

Dorothy hands in her book
the librarian checks the date
searches in a long wooden tray
packed tightly with library cards
takes one of them out
and gives it to Dorothy

thank you
Dorothy says

hurrying away
to choose another book

five minutes later
she takes the book
to the librarian
who opens it
takes out the card
slots it into Dorothy's card
puts it into the tray
picks up the date stamp
checks the numbers
presses it onto the ink pad
lowers it carefully
onto the open book
leans on it
lifts it up
closes the book
returns it
with a smile
to Dorothy

Dorothy thinks she would like
to be a librarian
when she grows up

thank you
she says
turning as she speaks

hurrying out
to wait for her mother
she holds the book

and its secrets
tight in her hand

its opening has to wait
until they are home again
only when she is alone
does she open her library book
always in the same way
as if she is stepping
from dry land
onto a rowing boat
that dips and sways
on the water
only then does she turn
to the first page
and smooth it with her hand
and start to read

5.

if the morning was fine
Annie would announce
that she was going out
to inspect her estate

by which she meant
her little back garden

after books
the garden was Dorothy's
favourite place

gardening
after reading
her favourite occupation

the garden
was where mother and daughter
were most comfortable together

when either of them spoke
it was to herself
the other
a silent
invisible
listener

if the morning was wet
Annie would say
rain before seven
fine before eleven
she was always right
the saying a charm
like touching wood
or throwing salt
over your shoulder

the mother
does not teach the daughter
how to garden
the daughter
learns
by watching

she watches the woman's hands
that might have been a man's

grasping the handles
of forks and spades
watches her fingers
strong and capable
roughened with
milking
scrubbing
pumping
fingers that look   ·
as if they belong
with the roots and tubers
under the soil

she learns
what the two leaves of a seedling
will grow into
what clues a leaf gives
to the colour of a flower
when to plant
when to prune
when to lift
when to hoe
when to rake
when to dig

more even than her mother
she loves anything that grows
as she loved
the weeds
that grew
in the cracks
of the pavement
outside the shop

she loves to read
and she loves to garden
the garden like a book
is another secret world
where she feels safe

6.

what's that you're reading?
Mr Leeming asked
Dorothy held up the book
so that he could see for himself

isn't it a bit old for you?

she looked down at the book on her lap
she didn't think it was too old for her
she had read it before
and was enjoying it again
but she didn't say that

she didn't say anything

what are you now?
he asked
ten is it?
eleven?

she was eleven last month
Annie said
old enough to speak for herself
but she won't

never mind
Mr Leeming said
she's shy
nothing wrong with that
better than talking out of turn
I like shyness in a girl

go on upstairs with your book
Annie said
Mr Leeming and me
have things to talk about
that don't concern you

Dorothy did as she was told
she lay on her bed
her book
propped on the pillow
her head
propped on her hands
safe again

go on then
Annie said
when she and Mr Leeming
were seated at the kitchen table
with the teapot between them
tell me the worst

the worst
Mr Leeming said
watching her pour the tea
is yet to come
the country is heading
for a depression

so am I
Annie said
I've hardly got enough
to live on as it is

unemployment is rising
Mr Leeming went on
interest rates are falling
it isn't over yet

Annie heaved a deep sigh
what's to become of us?
she said
me and the little one

what about the others?
Mr Leeming asked

they'll get by
Annie said
folk will always need coal
and there's still some
as can afford it

and Dinah?
how is our Dinah getting on?

engaged to be married

my compliments to the bride
Mr Leeming said
who's the lucky man?

you mean the one she's marrying
or the one that got away?

he's nearly three times her age
she went on
and he's got plenty of brass

Mr Leeming put a spoonful of sugar
into his tea
and stirred

the main thing
he went on
is not to touch your capital
interest rates might keep falling
but the one thing that is certain
is that they will rise again

aye
but when?

let me ask you one more question

I can guess what it is
Annie said
and you know what the answer is

Mr Leeming asked the question anyway

are you sure the quality of education
Dorothy is getting now
is so much better
than what she would get at the council school

as to justify what has always been
a significant item of expenditure
and is now even more so?

I'm not taking her away
Annie said

in which case
Mr Leeming said
all you can do is
reduce your outgoings
and move to a smaller house

7.

the house they moved to
had a backyard
but no garden
there was only one bedroom
and one bed
which they shared
but she didn't mind that

they were still in the village
they went shopping on Town Street
she could change her library books
and wait outside for her mother
there were no bare-bottom children
no barrels floating
in the cellar
no attic
with shameful secrets

just fields
and farms
rabbits hens cockerels
birds and wild flowers

Annie got two half-barrels
from somewhere
to go in the backyard
and a hanging basket
to go over the door

John Willy sent one of his men
to fix a bracket
for the hanging basket

it was autumn
so they planted tulips and wallflowers
in the half-barrels
and daffodils in the hanging basket
to give them something
to look forward to
in the spring

8.

get that red rud off
Annie said
meaning the lipstick
that Dorothy had put on

the other girls do it
Dorothy said

meaning the girls
at the chapel youth club

well you don't
Annie said
where did you get it anyway?

Dorothy said she had bought it
at the chemist

I shall have to give you less pocket money
if you've got enough to spend
on rubbish like that
get upstairs now
and wipe it off

Dorothy's body
was in more of a hurry
to grow up
than she was
she was shy
hated being looked at
but her body had other ideas

Annie had to explain things to Dorothy
sooner than she had expected
Dinah had not been so forward

if she had been able to
Dorothy would gladly
have swapped chests
with girls who envied hers

she was embarrassed
when boys
and sometimes men
looked at her
there
where she knew
she should never
let herself be touched

she didn't want to be touched
she didn't want to be looked at
she didn't want to be pretty
she wanted to be plain
like Jane Eyre

it wasn't vanity
that made her put on
the red rud that she now
not unwillingly
almost gratefully
wiped off
just that she wanted
to be like everyone else

she had no reason to be vain anyway
her knees were fat
her hair was like rats' tails
she had to wear thick glasses
she wasn't even plain
she was ugly

9.

Dorothy tries hard
her spelling is good
she has a good vocabulary
she knows her tables
she is good at mental arithmetic
she is average in most other subjects
her weakest subjects are art and needlework
she is quiet and conscientious

Annie read the report
and gave it back to her
without comment

10.

they're hiring at Rushworth's
Annie said
you'd better go
see if they'll give you a job

Rushworth's made tin toys
Dorothy joined a small army
of girls on an assembly line
you'll soon learn
they told her
but by the end of the week
the foreman came to the conclusion
that she wouldn't

I couldn't keep up
she explained
when she came home
on Friday evening
the foreman kept me back
when the others went
to get their wages
I told him it was because of my eyes
he said he was sorry
but the first week
was just a try-out
so I couldn't get paid

she started to cry
I'll try somewhere else
she said

Annie shook her head
you'd better just stop at home with me

11.

Dorothy's body forged ahead
leaving her to keep up as best she could

the country's depression
and Annie's
kept pace with each other

Annie took to her bed
and stopped talking

silence descended on the little house

Dorothy read without paying attention
often she would reach
the end of a chapter
and have to go back
and read it again
because she hadn't taken any of it in

sometimes the silence lasted a few days
sometimes a week
sometimes two
but always
each time it ended
it was as if it had never happened

they went shopping again
they went to chapel
Annie cooked
Dorothy gardened
and nothing was said

the silence always ended
but nothing was ever said

12.

Rowland wants to take me to the pictures

does he now?

Annie knew Rowland from chapel
which he attended with his mother
stepfather
and half-brother
his real father's name
was on the war memorial
not that she had ever seen it

what did you tell him?

Rowland played the piano at Sunday school
he played properly from music
not like the lodger at the shop

I said I didn't know

he could play the organ too
one Sunday when the organist was poorly
he stood in for him
nobody would have known
if the minister hadn't said
everyone turned round
and looked at him

you should have said no

he was older than her
he was an apprentice somewhere
but he was still a boy
he was supposed to be good at drawing
not like her
he went to night school for it

I didn't know what to say

she and her mother
had been to the pictures twice
since it opened on Town Street
they had laughed a lot at the first one
which had Charlie Chaplin in it
there was someone playing the piano
to go with what was happening
it reminded her of the lodger
the next one was a talkie
with jazz music
it had an American singer
called Al Jolson in it
blacking his face up
to look like a negro
someone took him off
at the chapel concert
they couldn't sing as well as him
but they made everyone laugh

if he means it
he'll ask you again

there was a boy called Percy
who she quite liked
he came to the chapel youth club sometimes
but he didn't go to chapel
he played the trombone
in the Salvation Army band
she had seen him once
marching all the way down Town Street
to the Green
looking smart in his uniform
she thought it must be hard
to march and keep in step

and keep blowing
and sliding in and out
all at the same time
Rowland said playing the organ
was harder than playing the piano
because you had to play
with your feet
as well as your hands
but she thought
playing and marching
must be harder

what shall I say if he does?

her mother didn't know Percy
because he didn't go to chapel
she knew Rowland
and she knew his mother
and his stepfather
who mended watches

that's up to you

Rowland
was nice enough

you mean I can if I want?

it would be nice
to see another film

just mind you don't
sit on the back row

one evening at the youth club
Percy brought his trombone with him
he showed them how to play it
some of the boys had a go
but none of them could do it properly
it just sounded as if
they were making rude noises
and everybody laughed

he played some hymn tunes
but the one everyone liked best was
When The Saints Go Marching In
everyone was tapping their feet
and some of the girls sang along
some of them even danced

they all clapped when he finished
and he took a bow
in a funny sort of way
that made them laugh
everyone wanted him to play again

he asked Rowland to join in
but Rowland said he didn't know it
Percy said it was easy
he went over to the piano
and played three chords
you just keep playing these
he said
Rowland said it's all right

I'd rather just listen
Dorothy thought it was because
he could only play
if he had the music
not like the lodger
he could have done it

when Percy was playing
and everyone was tapping their feet
and clapping in time to the music
she looked at Percy
then at Rowland
and decided she liked Percy best
Rowland wasn't even tapping his feet
in fact he didn't seem
to be enjoying it
at all

14.

well well well
Dinah said to her
when she made one of her
occasional visits
Mam says you've got a boyfriend
she says she knows when he's coming
because she can hear him
walking down the street
tapping his stick

only joking
what's his name?

Percy

that's not what Mam said

what's this about a lad called Percy?
Annie said

nothing
our Dinah was being horrible
I made it up

Rowland's the lad for you
you won't do any better
so don't go straying

do you hear me?

15.

Dorothy stopped going to the chapel youth club
she would have stopped going to chapel
if she could
but her mother would have wanted
to know why

a girl at the youth club asked
if it was true
Rowland and Percy
had a fight over her
she hoped it wasn't
but she didn't know

she forgot about it
when her mother told her
they were going to move

Mr Leeming had been right
the interest rate was rising
things were looking up
don't be too hasty though
he said
when she told him her plans
the world is still a very uncertain place
my advice to you
is to stay where you are

but this time she went her own way

the girl ought to have
a bed of her own now
she said

he could not disagree
and contented himself
with reminding her
not to spend all her capital

Dorothy and her mother
went together to look at houses
and found one
they liked
with two bedrooms
a small one at the front
and a bigger one at the back

when John Willy's men
carried their things
from the horse and cart
into the house
Dorothy was surprised
to see them putting her things
in the back bedroom

that's wrong
she said
mine's the small one at the front

nay miss
they said
that's what t' missis told us

you must have heard wrong
Dorothy said

the old one lit a cigarette
and sent the young one downstairs
to see who was right

tha's wrong miss
he said when he came back
she's at front
tha's at back

a cup o' tea 'd be nice
the old one said
throwing his cigarette out of the window
onto the back garden

Rowland and his mother
came for tea
on Saturday afternoons

after tea
their mothers talked
sending Rowland and Dorothy
out to the garden
if it wasn't raining

Rowland suggested
going for a walk
but Dorothy could not be persuaded

they were not walking out
and she didn't want anyone
to think they were

one Saturday afternoon
there was a special tea
at Rowland's house
to which Annie and Dorothy were invited

Rowland's stepbrother was there
as well as his mother and his stepfather
and his uncle George and aunty Mavis
on his mother's side
and his uncle Sam and aunty Elsie
on his father's side

the cause of the special tea
was the end of Rowland's apprenticeship
at the printer's in Leeds
where his uncle George worked

it was the first time
Aunty Elsie had met Dorothy
after tea she took her by the arm
and led her out to the garden
Dorothy would rather have stayed inside
with her mother
than listen to Aunty Elsie
talking about her favourite nephew

the firm takes advantage of him
she said
getting him to draw pictures
for sheet music covers
without paying him
he's such a good artist
he must have saved them a fortune
fair enough
he's doing it on their time
but that's not the point
anyone else would have to be paid
Rowland has a talent
a special talent
nobody taught him
he was born with it
his headmaster could see it
he wanted him to go
to the grammar school
but his mother couldn't see the point
seeing as her brother George

could get him apprenticed
Mr Robinson did his best
to try to persuade them
but they weren't interested
don't get me wrong
they're nice people
both of them
but they're not well educated
it would have been different
if my brother had lived
such a waste
him and millions more
I've been told you lost your father
to the Spanish flu
a lot went that way
that's something you and Rowland
have in common
you were both too young
to remember them
Rowland can't remember anything
about Walter
but he's so like him
the older he gets
the more I see my brother in him

Dorothy wondered why
Rowland had never told her
about the sheet music covers
she asked him about them
the next time he came to tea

Rowland said
shall I bring some to show you?

a few days later
Rowland learned
that his great-aunt Betty had died
and remembered him in her will
he was now the landlord
of a row of terraced houses
each with paying tenants

a man of property
Annie said

when Rowland remembered
to bring his pictures
he sat beside her on the settee
and showed them to her
one by one

she liked them
but she didn't like it
when he tried
to put his arm round her

keep your hands to yourself
she said

17.

the rent from Rowland's cottages
was modest
the terrace was old
the tenants poor
but now that he was a journeyman

earning a man's wage
it was enough
to knock a few weeks off the time
it took him to save
for an engagement ring

before he bought it
he wrote to Dorothy's mother
asking for her daughter's hand in marriage
she wrote back
saying she had no objection

the ring was in his pocket
when he knelt down
and asked her
to marry him

she had been afraid
it would come to this

I like you Rowland
she said
but I don't love you

dejected
he wrote again
to her mother

Dorothy has turned me down
he wrote
what can I do?

leave it to me
Annie wrote back

adding in a postscript
ask her again next Saturday

he did
and Dorothy did what her mother
told her to do
and said yes

Girl

Heather was born
during the war

Rowland got the news
by telegram
from a friend
who could afford
only one word

GIRL

he got leave
came home
on the train
to see her
so excited
so eager
to see his daughter
that he left his rifle
on the train

if the guard
hadn't spotted it
and given it
to a porter
on the platform
he would have found himself
on a charge

they decided
to call her
Heather
because she was born
on 12th August
the Glorious Twelfth
when grouse shooting begins
on the moors
where the purple heather grows

Dorothy and her mother
looked after the little one
for the rest of the war
she was nearly four
when Rowland came home
from Italy

in the first year of their marriage
they had lived with Annie
until Rowland found her
impossible to live with
testing his Christian charity
beyond what turned out
to be its limit

his efforts to make her laugh
with his impressions
of Charlie Chaplin
(the bow-legged walk
the walking stick)
Stan Laurel
(the head-scratching
the daft grin)
Arthur Askey

(the catchphrases
hello playmates
move along the car please)
failed to rouse her
from her grim silence

he gave up
finally
and applied
for a council house

there was a waiting list
but it wasn't very long
their new house was
close enough to her mother
for Dorothy
far enough from his mother-in-law
for Rowland

when war was declared
a few months later
Rowland wondered whether
the council house
had been a mistake

will you be all right on your own?

it's near enough
for Mum to visit
she said

don't let her move in
he said
you know what she's like

don't worry about me
she said
I can manage

he worried when he was
on the train to Wrexham
for basic training
but when he had his first leave
his wife seemed happy
and his mother-in-law
no worse than before

when he came back
for his next leave
from Croydon
it seemed as if Dorothy
had missed him
almost as much as he
had missed her

their wedding night
was repeated
with more success

a few weeks later
she wrote to tell him
that it had been
even more successful
than he thought

2.

he wrote to her every day during the war
every day for six years
from the day he left for Wrexham
to the day he came back from Italy

she wrote back
but not every day

mother and grandmother
took care of the little one
the war was far away
only one bomb was dropped
near enough to be heard
a mile and a half away
at the forge
killing two men

life in the village
went on in not quite the usual way
but they got used to it

they planted vegetables
instead of flowers
made do with powdered eggs
listened to the wireless
ITMA
Forces' Favourites
Workers' Playtime

on Sundays they took it in turns

to go to chapel
or stay at home with the baby

Rowland told her in his letters
how much he liked Italy
especially Rome
where he arrived when it was liberated
and stayed until the war ended

someone had told him
he would have a better chance
of following his trade
if he joined up early
he joined the Royal Engineers
the Helio Division
printing maps by the light of the sun
which didn't shine much
in Wrexham or Croydon
but shone in abundance
in Italy

he wrote in his letters
about the ruined villages
they passed on the march to Rome
Rome was in ruins too
but the people greeted them
with smiles and tears

he told her about an Italian woman
he met at their camp
and made friends with
her name was Maria
she belonged to a church group
who helped to serve meals to the troops

she was a Catholic
which was not something
Methodists generally approved of
but everyone in Italy was a Catholic
so she didn't really have a choice

this unmarried Italian woman
who befriended her husband
claiming to see similarities between
Methodism and Catholicism
that had hitherto gone unnoticed
taking him to see an opera
when he told her
he had never seen one
could easily have aroused
Dorothy's jealousy
if she hadn't known Rowland
well enough to know
that he could be trusted

unless it was just that
she didn't really care

3.

she was playing with Heather
Sandy McPherson on the wireless
playing the organ
she hummed along
made Heather's doll
dance to the music
while they waited for Grandma

come on Heather
she said at last
let's go and see where she is

with Heather in the pushchair
she set off to walk up the hill

the door was unlocked
she left Heather outside
and went in

Mum
it's me
are you all right?

Mum
what are you doing there?

Mum
what's wrong?

there was no doubt about it

her mouth open
she lay on the kitchen floor
where she had dropped
like a bag of coal

Dorothy went out again
and closed the door

Grandma can't come today
she said
she wheeled the pushchair
up the hill
hearing her mother say
for the umpteenth time
you can't go anywhere
in this village
without going up a hill

she stopped at the doctor's house
lifted Heather out of the pushchair
and went in

the doctor's secretary
seated at her neat desk
telephone
writing pad
trays for letters
looked up and smiled

seeing who it was
Dorothy with her baby
but without her mother
her expression changed

Dorothy
she said
is everything all right?

4.

is it always like this here?

he meant
the cold and the rain
that was all

he was glad
to be home again
with his wife and daughter
he took photographs
of both of them
on his new camera
using wartime blackout
to make the kitchen
into a darkroom
developing the glass plates
and making prints

he made a hobby horse
for Heather
painted it in bright colours
photographed her sitting on it
in black and white

he loved to watch
the little girl
when she was sleeping
he would go upstairs
and stand by her bed
leaning over her

looking down at her face
a picture of perfect peace
like the water babies in the book
in their watery heaven

wedding nights
revived and repeated
were not always
entirely satisfactory
but satisfactory or not
one of them
proved successful

he settled into his old job again
some old faces were missing
but most were still there

the girls in the office were new
knock knock
one of them said
he looked blank

you have to say
who's there?
knock knock

who's there?

Nicholas
now you have to say
Nicholas who?

Nicholas who?

knickerless girl gets cold in winter

he repeated the joke
when he got home
I suppose you heard that
when you were in the army

no
he said
it was a girl in the office
a new one
they were never like that before

when the boy came
they called him Stewart Neil
Heather was Jean Heather
they had wanted her
to have two names
and chose Jean for euphony
it was the same for the boy
the second name for each of them
was the one they were known by
the first a mere appendage
like the silent letter
at the beginning of some words

5.

when the war was over
and Rowland back at work
it wasn't long before he became

a five-pound-a-week man
in charge of the department
where as a boy of fourteen
he had started as an apprentice

we could get a motor car
Dorothy said

a second-hand Austin 7
was the obvious choice
learning to drive
with his brother-in-law
in the passenger seat
easy enough on roads
where you were as likely
to have to overtake
a horse and cart
as another motor car

when he took the driving test
the examiner pointed to a house
and told him to stop outside
wait here
he said
I won't be long
when he got back in the car
he explained the reason
for the unscheduled stop
my braces had bust
he said
I had to go in and change them
nothing to do with the test
you've passed by the way

the little black car
with the registration APY127
known to its owner
as Appy
was one of the first
to be seen on their street

if they saw a car coming
children playing on the street
would shout car!
run to the pavement
and watch it go slowly past

car-spotting
was nearly as popular
as trainspotting

it was Appy now
not the train
who took them to the seaside
for their summer holiday
always to the same town
on the Yorkshire coast
staying at the same boarding house
run by Albert and Audrey
who used to live in the village

Heather and her new little brother
played on the beach all week
paddling and building sandcastles
Dorothy and Rowland sat nearby
on deckchairs hired by the hour
watching them play

when it rained they sat
in the shelter on the front
watching the sea
or went to a café
for tea and ice cream
or to the penny arcade

there were donkey rides on the beach
and for a special treat
a donkey ride back to the boarding house

Dorothy said
why don't you get a job here?
but Rowland had lived in the village
all his life and had no wish to leave

anyway he had other plans
of which he had said nothing to anyone
except a friend at work
they had been apprentices together
separated by the war
now together again
both five-pound-a-week men
both restless
after six years in the army
looking forward to coming home
feeling somehow disappointed
by what they found when they got there

it was not as they had remembered it
not what they had expected

knowing nothing of this
Dorothy was disappointed in him
thought he lacked ambition
and told him so

6.

Heather passed the 11+
as her teachers expected
and in September 1952
went to the grammar school
not the nearest
but the oldest
1575 on the school badge

her journey on the bus
was shorter than her mother's
had been on the tram
and the school was a lot better

a quiet and shy child
taking after her mother
more than her father
she was sometimes picked on
at the big school

in her first term
coming home on the bus
a girl grabbed her school beret
and threw it out of the window

she went with her father

to look for it
still sobbing
when they found it
at the side of the road

in her second term
she had earache

ear drops from the chemist
held in with plugs of cotton wool
made no difference
except for making it
hard to hear the teachers

Dorothy took her to the doctor
who said it would soon clear up
and told her to continue with the treatment
but the earache got worse

complaining at school one day
about a bad headache
she was sent home on the bus
with a girl who lived on the same street

Dorothy took her to the doctor again
the doctor shone a torch in her ears
and sent her back to the waiting room
while he made a phone call

Dorothy and Heather waited
until the secretary came in
and said they could go home
the doctor would see them there

he came in the evening
with a specialist
whose angry voice
could be heard downstairs

Heather was taken by ambulance to the hospital
where she died the next morning

7.

Rowland had gone to the hospital
in the ambulance with Heather
and came back in the morning
on the bus

without a telephone
Dorothy had to wait
most of the morning
before she found out
what had happened

she's in heaven now
Rowland said
when he came in

Dorothy said nothing
clamping her mouth shut
on her guilt

it was her fault
all her fault
pretending it was nothing serious
she should have known better

I couldn't stop crying on the bus
Rowland said
the conductor let me stand on the platform

he sat down
at the kitchen table
resting his forehead
on his hands

she stood
at the window
looking out

neither of them noticed
the five-year-old boy
standing in the doorway
watching them

8.

Heather died on 17th March
St Patrick's Day
and was cremated a week later

it was a very quiet affair
Rowland's aunty Elsie had told him
not to take pride in his grief

this least ostentatious of men
understood what she meant
and grieved in private

the little boy went to school as usual
while his parents and a few relatives
said goodbye to his sister

at playtime he lay down
in the playground
and curled into a ball

one of the old teachers
who had once taught his father
picked him up and carried him inside

that night when his father
put him to bed
he said his prayers as usual

God bless Mummy and Daddy and Heather
and Grandma and Grandpa
and make Neil a good boy amen

when he had finished
he wondered whether he should
have left Heather out

opening his eyes
he said
we'll have to forget her now

his father said no
we must remember her
and kissed him goodnight

she was never forgotten
they all remembered her

but nothing was ever said

until many years later
when Rowland was long gone
and there were only the two of them left

9.

Aunty Elsie brought
a letter from the council
to show to Rowland

it was a compulsory purchase order
for the row of terraced houses
his great-aunt Betty had left him

it's the slum clearance
she said
you'll get compensation

she pointed to the amount
they're worth more than that
she said

Rowland was not unhappy
to have to give up
being a landlord

especially now that he knew
he had been charging rent
on houses that were slums

but he had never felt
that he earned the rent
in the way that he earned his wages

the compensation from the council
turned out to be just enough
for a deposit on a new house

10.

the house they bought
was a pre-war semi near the station
at the other end of the village
with a front garden
as big as the old back garden
and a back garden
bigger than both put together

it was a new start for them
with a new garden for Dorothy
leaving behind the house
where Heather was born
and Neil and another child
that was lost before it was born

Rowland drove to work every day
Neil went to school
Dorothy stayed at home

milk and coal were delivered
at first by horse and cart
then by milk float and lorry

Rowland called with a shopping list
at the butcher and the baker
on his way home from work
he took a list every week to the grocer
who did deliveries in his van
newspapers were delivered every day
by the paper boy
and Dorothy stayed at home

11.

one day when Dorothy was
out in the back garden
the woman who lived next door
called to her over the fence

I've just realised where I've seen you before
she said
I thought I knew you
I used to see you in the village
you were always with your mother
weren't you?

when Rowland came home from work
Dorothy said she would like to plant
some climbing roses
and jasmine
and honeysuckle
and clematis
in the back garden
it would need some trellis
down the side of the garden

it would make it more private

wanting to deny her nothing
he got someone in to do it
and Dorothy was able to go on
gardening in peace

12.

she knew
from the moment Rowland
started telling her about his plan
that it would end in ruin

she told him so
as vehemently and persistently
as the prophetess Cassandra
warned the king her brother of Troy's ruin

when the loan was secured
against the house they lived in
she saw a vision of bailiffs
and wrung her hands

when premises were found
papers signed
and the first rent paid
she grew angry

hearing voices downstairs
Neil got out of bed
and stood on the landing

what are you arguing about?

Rowland put him back to bed
we're just talking
he said
go back to sleep now

13.

the news Rowland told Dorothy
when it was too dark for her
to stay out in the garden
was meant to reassure her

they were getting so many orders
he said
it was hard to keep up with them
they would have to take on
somebody else before long
it was too much for the two of them

she listened without comment
there was no doubt in her mind
any more than there was in Cassandra's
that ruin would come in the end

but there was no point in arguing
you know best
she said
I don't know why you bother telling me

14.

while her husband was running the business
Dorothy was running the home
while he was moving the business
to new premises in Leeds
she was scrimping and saving
to pay off the mortgage on the house
while he was paying himself more
she was managing on less
while the business was paying for a new car
and he was out driving it
getting home late at night
she was at home all day

their ten-year-old son did the shopping now
on the bogie his father made for him
out of pram wheels and a plank

the weekly delivery of groceries
was no longer made by the grocer in his van
but by Neil sitting on his bogie
steering with the rope
using his feet as brakes
with the groceries in a box behind him

the three of them lived in different worlds
hers was the only real one
her husband's and her son's
were dream worlds
which was as it should be for one
but not for the other

all she could do was pay off the mortgage
and save them all from the ruin
that was bound to occur
when Rowland woke up

15.

Dorothy was easily persuaded
to let her son take a day off school
whenever he said he was feeling poorly

she knew he was only pretending
knew she ought to make him get up
and send him off to school

but she liked to know he was upstairs
sitting up in bed reading a book
while she was getting on with the housework

she liked it when she heard him shout
Mum! Mum!
can I have something to write with?

all she had ever learned
had been learned at home reading books
never at school

Neil was clever
his sister had passed the 11+
and so would he

she only wished she could get him
off *Just William*
and onto *David Copperfield*

his father said she spoiled him
Heather used to say he was her favourite
but what harm had it done him?

she let him stay in bed
and wrote a note for him
to give to his teacher in the morning

16.

they had been invited to tea
by the parents of a little girl
Neil had made friends with at school

her name was Beryl
she was new
a pretty girl with curly brown hair

it turned out that her father
had known his father in the war
both of them printers

when he realised who it was
Rowland didn't want to go
he had never liked him much

for the five years since Heather died
Dorothy had never left the house
so the invitation would have to be declined

it was for their son's sake perhaps
that she surprised him by saying
she thought they ought to go

when tea was served
the men talked more than their wives
and their children not at all

after tea the men smoked
the children went out to play
and the women washed up

while they did
something made Dorothy
start talking about Heather

it was as if she heard herself
telling the story of Heather's death
and her grief

how she blamed herself
though her husband told her
it wasn't her fault

but it always was
wasn't it
a mother's fault

she was glad
when the washing up was done
and the story ended

two women
strangers

never to meet again

one woman's story
taken home
put away

17.

Rowland had his first stroke
one evening when he stood up
to turn the television on
lost his balance
and fell over

are you all right?
Dorothy said
hearing the noise
coming in when he didn't reply
finding him on the floor

his speech was slurred
she rang the doctor
the doctor came at once
and told him
he'd had a stroke

only a little one
he said
you'll get over it
I'll come back in the morning
to see how you are

your dad's had a stroke
Dorothy said
when Neil came down later
from doing his homework
only a little one

all he knew about strokes
was the first line
of a story by James Joyce
there was no hope for him this time
it was the third stroke

this was the first
he thought
putting the television on
so there was nothing
to worry about

18.

coming home for his dinner one day
opening the kitchen door
the first thing Rowland noticed
was the smell of gas
the second was his wife
with her head in the oven

he turned off the gas
and tried to lift her up

leave me alone
she said

bewildered
he left her on the floor
and went to look for his son
who was back from university
for the long summer holiday

I've just found your mum
with her head in the oven
he said

Neil looked up from his book
and stared at his father

Rowland went back to the kitchen
to find his wife sticking a fork in the potatoes
to see if they were ready

you're in my way
she said
leave me alone

they sat down at the table and waited
until she brought them their dinner

you'll have to excuse me
she said
I'm going to lie down

they helped themselves
to mashed potato liver and onions
listening to the news on the wireless

your mother's in a bad way
what's wrong with her?

she worries about money
she just makes things worse

after dinner father and son
went their separate ways
one back to work
the other to see a friend

when Rowland got back from work
he found his wife lying on the bed
a tumbler and a bottle of whisky
on the bedside table
her eyes were open
but she didn't seem to see him

he took the bottle downstairs
put it back in the sideboard
with the others that had been given to him
over several Christmases
by customers and suppliers
and never opened

he went back upstairs
and found his wife
in the bathroom
being sick
he wiped her mouth
helped her downstairs

what's going on?
his son asked
when he came back
from his friend's house

his father told him
stay with your mum
he said
I'm going up to change the bed

Neil stood in front of her
where she sat on the settee
like a pile of dirty washing
like a bird fallen out of the nest

I hate you
he said

I want my mummy
she said
where's my mummy?

19.

the doctor prescribed tablets
to calm Dorothy's nerves
the same doctor
who prescribed tablets
for Rowland's blood pressure

not the doctor who had failed
to diagnose Heather's illness
that doctor had given up his practice
and gone away
blaming himself for her death

you're a worrier

the new doctor said
your own worst enemy
keeping everything in
it's better to talk
is there no one you can talk to?

because he was new
and didn't know her
and told her straight out
that she was her own worst enemy
which nobody had ever said before
but which she knew to be true
she told him about Heather
and how she had been a recluse
ever since she died

when she told him she had no friends
he didn't believe her
there must be someone you can talk to
he said
the person she thought of was Mrs Briggs
who lived next door but two
but she's just lost her husband
she said
she won't want me bothering her

you might be surprised
he said
ask her round for a cup of tea
show her your garden
your garden is lovely by the way
I don't think I've ever seen one like it
it certainly puts mine to shame

when she was taking her tablets
and Rowland was taking his
and it was just the two of them again
Neil being back at university
life went on as it had before

what she had done
had only made things worse
as it always did

her father must have known
this one's different
he said
not like the others

there was nothing Dinah couldn't do
she was a wonderful seamstress
she made all her own clothes
she could turn her hand to anything
when women were needed
to fill men's jobs during the war
she worked as a bus conductor
she and her second husband
had a bungalow near Scarborough
her garden won prizes
she kept hens
the last time they went to see them
when they were on holiday with Neil
Rowland asked if she could spare a dozen
she went out to get them

that'll be two shillings
she said
I'll give it to you when we go
Dorothy said quickly
in case Rowland thought she was joking

I knew when you asked
that she'd want paying
she said when they were back in the car
there's no sentiment with Dinah
any more than there is with John

they're not like you
she thought
which is why
she's got a bungalow in Scarborough
and he's got a Jaguar
and your business is failing

she did her best
not to make things worse for him
if they could just keep going
until the mortgage was paid off
he didn't want to talk about it
he didn't want to worry her
but she could tell things were bad

sometimes when he'd had his dinner
instead of going back to work
he would sit in his armchair
loosen his trousers
and close his eyes
shouldn't you be going back?
she would say

and he would open his eyes
and sometimes he would get up
and fasten his trousers
and go back to work
and sometimes he would say
they could manage without him

21.

the next stroke
was serious enough
for them to send an ambulance
to take him to hospital
where he stayed for a few days
until they got him on his feet
and talking again

the mortgage was still not paid off
but as things turned out
it didn't really matter

he sat downstairs one morning
for a meeting with the other director
and the company chairman
he was tired when they left
and went back to bed
he asked her to come up
and sit with him
he told her she had nothing
to worry about now

I've resigned
he said
I've had to give up all my shares
not that they were worth much
so I've got no assets
but I've got no liabilities either
and we've got the house

reaching out for her hand
but not reaching it
he looked at her
and smiled
a little wearily
everything's all right
he said
there's nothing to worry about

she left him to rest
and went downstairs
to be on her own

22.

the business had failed
as she had always known it would
it had lasted ten years
he would have to find work now

not well enough yet
he set up his easel
sat on a stool in front of it
and began to paint

he painted watercolours
of drawings in his sketchbook
made on days out in the Dales
with picnics in lay-bys

his speech improved
though it was still a little slurred
he had a slight limp
but he walked well enough

he bought oil paints
a set of brushes
and a palette knife
and joined the local art club

he enjoyed Neil's company
when he was home from university
and let him do the driving
when they went out

the holidays at Cambridge
were longer than the terms
Rowland's recuperation
was like a long holiday

Neil went out one day
for a drive on his own
and came back
with a walking stick

it was too long
he had to saw it
to the right length
before his father could use it

Dorothy remembered
the Charlie Chaplin impressions
that made everyone laugh
even her mother sometimes

the walking stick helped him
regain his confidence
and with it his pride
despite an occasional fall

I've had an idea
he said one evening
why don't we get a little shop
somewhere in the Dales?

what do you know about running a shop?
she said
of all the daft ideas!
and he let it drop

23.

it was young Mr Edward
who answered Rowland's call
the original son
in the firm of Edward Bainbridge & Son
though he was Rowland's age now
with a son of his own in the business

everyone was surprised
he said
you had such a good name in the trade

don't worry
there'll be something for you
leave it with me
how long can you last?
are you all right for a month or two?
I heard you'd not been well
are you all right now?

Dorothy thought he was too trusting
how do you know he means it?
people say all kinds of things
more promises are made than kept

Rowland said he'd known him for years
he's a decent chap
he said
he had wanted to cheer her up
he tried to put his arm around her
but she shook it off
he was used to that
but it still made him feel sad

24.

when their son got married
Dorothy and Rowland
were pleased for different reasons
Rowland because he thought
Neil had found a good wife
Dorothy because she thought
he had a proper family now
which theirs had never been

she kept these thoughts to herself
and was comforted by them
it was a load off her mind

it was a long drive for Rowland
everything was hard for him now
they left early to avoid the traffic
but the Pennine roads were bleak
even on a summer morning
just mist and stone
and sheep that looked like stone
mile after lonely mile
he kept his eyes on the road
she kept hers on the map
neither had much to say

they arrived without mishap
and stayed side by side
at the marriage in the register office
and the reception at the bride's family home
Rowland was able to relax now
enjoy the meal and the speeches
take pride in his son
and feel a kind of contentment
as in something achieved
a handing over
Dorothy felt a different kind of contentment
more like an ending than a beginning
and worried about the journey back

after the meal and the speeches
waiting to see them off on their honeymoon
saying goodbye to everyone
it was later than they had planned

when they set off to drive home
it was still light when they left
but night was falling on the moors

are you sure this is right?
Dorothy pushed her glasses up
I can't see
it doesn't look right to me
don't say we're lost
everything looks different at night
you'd better stop and look at the map
I'll go on a bit further

the only light on the moors
was the light of their headlamps
on the road ahead
moving with them
through the darkness

on they went
Rowland driving slowly
looking for a landmark
something to tell him where he was

Dorothy looked straight ahead
the map forgotten

on they went
slower and slower
while Dorothy prayed

what are we going to do?

suddenly a light shone in the darkness
a bright light that filled the sky
as if someone had lit a beacon

I know where we are now
he said
we aren't lost
it's all right

25.

Rowland looked young again
driving up to Durham
in the spring
to visit Neil and his wife
it was almost
Dorothy thought
as if they were going on holiday
with Neil in the back

it's a straight road
he said
A1
Great North Road
I've done it many a time
as far as Scotch Corner
Durham's not much further

they stayed for one night
Neil took them in his car
from their bungalow
on a housing estate

outside Durham
to the city itself
over the river
up a steep road
to the marketplace
where a policeman
on traffic duty
waved them on
up another steep road
to the top of the hill
where they saw the castle
and the cathedral
with a broad green between them

after they parked the car
they walked along a cobbled street
with old houses on either side
gardens with old roses
old iron gates
an old water pump

everything's old here
Neil said

his father nodded
like me

the smile on his face
she thought
was the old one
the wry smile he had
when he was a young man

they went back to the car
drove back down
to the bottom of the hill
left the car in a car park
walked back up
mother and daughter-in-law in front
father and son following

mother heard something
looked round
saw father on the pavement
son helping him up
people stopping to look

is he all right?

it's too steep for him
she thought
he tries to keep up
then he falls

it's a shame

26.

young Mr Edward
kept his promise

quality control
he said
when he rang back
a fortnight later

by which time
Dorothy had lost
what little hope she had

have you heard of that?
we've been thinking about it
for a while now
it means having someone
to keep an eye on quality
all the way through the job
from start to finish
when you rang me
it was the first thing I thought of
I thought Rowland could do that
with his eyes closed
not the best way of putting it
but you know what I mean

27.

it's not a real job
he told her
it's just for show
I've got a little office
a white coat
and a clipboard
to make me look important

there was a note of resignation
in his voice
that was new
her heart went out to him

one evening
when there were some boys
riding bicycles
up and down the road
he went out and told them
to go and play on their own street
they went straightaway
but she felt sure
some of them lived there

she had never seen him
do anything like that before
he was the nicest
most good-tempered man
you could imagine
but now

she had made him like this
it was her fault
he should have married someone else

28.

you'd better send for the boy
Rowland said
lying in bed
recovering from what
the doctor said
had been a mild heart attack
not another stroke
as they had thought

how can I do that
when they haven't got a telephone?

he suggested sending a telegram
but she said that would only worry him

I'll tell him on Sunday
when he rings

your dad's had a heart attack
she said
when Neil rang as usual
at eleven o'clock
on Sunday morning
just a mild one
nothing to worry about

I want to see him
Neil said
I'll drive down now

she told him there was no need
he's sitting up in bed
she said
he's doing fine
you don't want to be driving
all that way
on a day like this
what if it snows?

it was foggy outside the telephone box
a typical November day
cold and grey

she persuaded him to stay at home
you'll be seeing him at Christmas
she said
there's no need to come now
he'd rather you stayed at home
than drive all the way down here
he's getting over it now
there's nothing to worry about

Friday 13th December 1974

Dorothy looks out of her kitchen window
on a cold wintry morning, soil frozen,
grass silvery, each blade sharpened by frost.
A robin perches on the bird table,
cocks its head, sees her through the glass, flies off.
Upstairs, Rowland is sitting up in bed,
eating from the tray she put on his knee,
cornflakes, toast, marmalade, tea, no sugar,
as prescribed on the dietary notes
the doctor left behind last time he called.
He stopped smoking, says he doesn't miss it,
but she knows if it hadn't been for her
he would never have started. All my fault,
she thinks, like everything else. I'm to blame.
A silly girl, thinking a man should smoke,
liking the way men held their cigarettes,
thinking it made them look, you know, sexy.
Not that I knew anything about that,
or even liked it much when I found out.
He would have been better off without me.
I've never been a proper wife to him.
I would have been better staying at home
with Mum, looking after her until she died.
Dad said I was different, so why did she
try to make me be like everyone else?
I was born to be the daughter who stayed
at home, looked after Mum, died a spinster,
or went mad one night and burned the house down.

I'm not like Dinah, living happily
in Scarborough with husband number three,
no more than Rowland is like my brother
with his Jaguar and his big new house.
Rowland's an artist, not a businessman.
I've been no help to him, just made him smoke
and watched him suffer with one stroke
after another brought on by the stress
of running a business and living with me.
And when the business failed I was no use.
All I could see was us losing the house,
all I could do was try to kill myself,
or pretend to. It's all pretence with me.

She hears strange noises coming from upstairs.
"Are you all right?" A crash! That's his breakfast.
"I'm coming!" She goes up to the bedroom,
gets there in time to witness the last scene
of his agony. His face contorted,
struggling, sweating, his hands clenched. "Dorothy!"
His last word, he lets go, it is over.

She is alone, with another sorrow.
She has forgotten how to cry, her grief
stored up, set aside with each new sorrow.
She has never seen any of them cry,
mother, sister, brother. If they had tears
they were just for show, put on like mourning
at funerals. Real grief should be silent.
Free of her, Rowland has found peace at last.
All she wants now is to sit beside him
and be quiet and share his peacefulness,
such peacefulness as she will never find.

He loved her. She never wanted his love
but still he loved her. He was the Bible's
good and faithful servant, never repaid.
Blamed, criticised, turned away, never loved.
Until now, unless even now it is
not that, but something else, a debt paid off
with sorrow. She loved the daughter they lost,
loved Heather but never loved her father,
and she loves their son who has a wife now
and must soon be told of this new sorrow.
She should tell someone now, ring the doctor,
but all she wants is to find some peace here
in this silence, this new-found loneliness,
for she is alone now, truly alone.
Is he in heaven now, as he always
believed, as she would like to believe too?
His soul has left his body, but still lives,
both still present, though separated now.
Our immortal souls are not candle flames
to be snuffed out as if they never burned.
He was unwavering in his belief.
Heather will not be lonely in heaven,
he said. Her grandma is already there.
Are father and daughter together now?
Questions like these are disturbing her peace.
All she wants is to be quiet and still
in the emptiness that he leaves behind,
the empty space that will stay empty now,
like the space that Heather left when she died,
undisturbed by the noise that living makes.

She goes to the window, thinking to close
the curtains, but before she does she looks
down at her garden, as the robin might,
perched on a high branch of the lilac tree,
and sees in winter's cold stubborn beauty,
as in a glass, death's features at her back.
She draws the curtains, turns and on the bed
she sees again the young man she married.
Sitting on the bed by his side, she sees
his face pale and smooth again, his thin lips
about to smile and say something funny
to make her laugh, though now making her cry.

I'm all right

the doctor said he would break the news
to save her having to do it herself
she gave him her son's
and her brother's
telephone numbers

her brother came first
put his arms round her
sat down and said
we've all had it to deal with

he was a good man
he said
when she brought him a cup of tea

it was after six when her son came
he shook hands with his uncle
and introduced his wife
John shook hands with her
laughing at the difference
between them
her tiny hand swallowed up
in his capacious fist

he went home then
late for his dinner

her son and daughter-in-law
slept that night
in Neil's old bedroom
in a single bed
rarely slept in
since he left

Dorothy passed
her first night
as a widow
not yet quite alone

you go now
she says in the morning
I'm all right

her son drove his wife home
returned in the evening
and stayed for nearly a week
taking the compassionate leave
that his teaching contract entitled him to
and persuading the headmaster
to add the few days
that remained
before the holiday

I'm all right
she says
don't worry about me
but she was glad
not to be
quite alone
just yet

2

Uncle Sam
Rowland's real father's brother
is sobbing
loud and unrestrained
somewhere at the back
she can't see where he is
but she can hear him and wishes
he would show more self-control

in my Father's house are many mansions
if it were not so I would have told you
I go to prepare a place for you

hearing the minister's words
she feels a sob rising
holds it down
squeezing her son's hand

it takes him by surprise
he is not used to his mother
showing her feelings
he was surprised but pleased
that she took his hand
when they went in
the tightening of her grip
pleases him again
brief though it is

the funeral is at the crematorium
she has not been to chapel
since Rowland was expelled
for working on a Sunday

two senior members visited him at home
telling him to choose between
God and Mammon

he said
it was not like that
just that work
had to be done on time
and there was only him to do it

still they insisted
God or Mammon

he chose God
knowing that God would not object
if he had to work on a Sunday

but they knew
he had really chosen Mammon
and expelled him

he still said his prayers every night
kneeling on the floor beside the bed
his faith in human beings
might have been shaken
but not his faith in God

the years of being alone
begin a few days later
when her son leaves
to spend Christmas
with his wife and her family

she loses weight

one morning
out shopping
at the new supermarket
in the village
she feels something tickling her leg
it turns out to be
her knickers falling down
what can she do
but step out of them
and put them in her shopping bag?

she loses touch

one morning
she goes out
to pay her gas bill
at the gas board office
on Town Street
the shop assistant
looks at the bill
that she holds out
and tells her

with a smile
that the gas board
is no longer there
in fact
he says
it no longer exists

looking round
she sees
that what was
the gas board
the last time she went
is now a shop
selling furniture

the young man
suggests she try
the post office
does she know
where that is?

she walks home
on the streets
that she used to know
feeling alone
and desolate

4.

she tries to carry on
as if nothing has happened
sticking to her old routine

it is important
she tells herself
to have a routine

the garden thaws
the March wind blows
the sparrows peck
the yellow crocuses
as they do every year

she forgets sometimes
that he has gone
thinks in the morning
of things to tell him
when he comes home
for his dinner
until she remembers
he will not be coming home

she walks to the nursery
to buy spring bedding
alyssum and lobelia
for edging
petunias marigolds snapdragons
to plant here and there
she scatters seeds
larkspur poppies godetia
and lets them grow
where they will

it is mainly out of habit
the garden does not give her pleasure
so much as remind her of the pleasure
it used to give

5

Mrs Briggs
retired primary school headmistress
her next-door neighbour but two
asks how she's getting on

I'm all right
she says
I'm getting used to it

Mrs Briggs says
if you want some company
just come round

after she has gone
Dorothy realises she should have
asked her in
not kept her talking
on the doorstep
she should have
made her a cup of tea
put some biscuits on a plate

the next time Mrs Briggs calls
she asks her in
you must think I'm rude
she says

Mrs Briggs says
don't worry
I know what it's like

Dorothy remembers
while she makes the tea
and gets the biscuits out
that Mrs Briggs lost her husband
two or three years ago
perhaps more

your garden's looking lovely again
Mrs Briggs says
looking out of the kitchen window
Harry always admired your garden

it's what keeps me going
Dorothy says

they drink their tea
and talk
and before she goes
Mrs Briggs says
it's nice to see you like this
don't forget to come round
any time you want a bit of company

when she's gone
Dorothy goes upstairs to lie on her bed
tired from the effort of talking
of pretending
that's all it is
she thinks
pretence
putting on an act
that's all

6.

Neil telephones
on Sunday afternoon
as usual
and tells her
he's got a new job
at a school not so far away
closer to his wife's parents too

when we move
we'll be able to come
and see you
more often

don't worry about me
she says
so long as you're all right
that's all that matters

he says he will be starting
his new job after Easter
leaving his wife behind
until she finishes her course

she's going to look for a job
at a school near mine
he says

she hears him putting
another coin in the slot

save your money
she says
there's no need
thank you for ringing

he says it will take a few weeks
to sort things out
he will come and see her
as soon as he can

I'll ring again next Sunday
he says

7.

the hedgerows are white
with blossom
Dorothy and Mrs Briggs
have gone for a walk
across the fields
to the next village
five miles
there and back

it's only time
Mrs Briggs says
time's a healer

Dorothy thinks it's the kind of thing
her mother used to say
but it never really worked for her
did it?

you can't cling onto the past
you have to let it go

was that her mother's mistake?
but how can you let things go
when they cling to you?

it's no use going over it all
Mrs Briggs says
wishing you'd done things differently
we all do it
but it's a vain endeavour
what's done is done
and there's nothing you can do
to change it

I know
Dorothy says
but how can you forget?

you can't
not altogether
just don't let it hold you back
there are good times ahead

I wish I could be like you
Dorothy says

just be yourself Dorothy
you're a very nice person
very thoughtful
perhaps you think
too much

Rowland said I was always frowning
he used to say
don't frown Dorothy

the footpath they are following
climbs up a long slope
the footpath narrows
Mrs Briggs goes in front
they walk in silence
until they reach
the brow of the ridge

they stop to get their breath back
and admire the view
the whole valley
spread out below
farms and hamlets sketched
between the fields

Harry loved this
Mrs Briggs says
it always brings back happy memories

why is it only sad memories
that come back to me?
Dorothy thinks

it's lovely
she says to Mrs Briggs
wishing she really meant it
thinking it's just words

her memories are overgrown
with guilt and shame
all they bring to mind
is the punishment she deserves
for the harm she has done

when they get back
Mrs Briggs invites her in
for a cup of tea
and a piece of cake

Dorothy thanks her
but declines the invitation
saying she is tired now
and needs to lie down

I've really enjoyed it
Mrs Briggs says
we must do it again

Dorothy walks along the road
and lets herself in
wishing she could feel
what she ought to feel
instead of pretending
pretending
pretending
always
pretending

8.

Neil asks his mother
to spend a weekend with him

his wife has a term to go
before she can join him
in the house he is renting
on a new housing estate
near his new school

he picks her up in his father's car
which is his car now
it is the first time
she has been in it
since Rowland died

sitting in the passenger seat again
brings back more unhappy memories
the only kind that stay with her now

the happy times
that Mrs Briggs tells her
she should remember
were a long time ago
sometimes she finds it hard
to believe they ever happened

my spirits won't rise
she thinks
knowing she will disappoint him
flatten him
as she flattened his father

he doesn't look like him
she thinks
but he has his spirit
never down for long
always rising
except at the end

she does her best
not to disappoint him
when he suggests
moving to a smaller house
nearer to him and his wife

the suggestion neither raises
nor lowers her spirits

he shows her the new school
the new town
the new shopping centre
the new park
the new lake

she does not even need to pretend
all she has to do is acquiesce

9.

Mrs Briggs tells her
it was kind of her son
to want her to be nearer
to him and his wife

but thinks she should wait

it's not a time for hasty decisions
she says
wait until they're settled
they've not been married long
you have friends here
you're not alone

Dorothy says
she doesn't want to be
a burden on anyone

Mrs Briggs says
you shouldn't think of it like that

I'm best on my own
I can't rise
I wish I could
but I can't

Mrs Briggs suggests
going for another walk

Dorothy shakes her head

it's very kind of you
she says
but I can't
I don't know why
I just can't

10.

she avoids going out
she gardens
does housework
eats very little
thinks it might be better
to put an end to a life
that is a regret to her
and a burden to others
lies awake at night

one day she finds the number
for the Samaritans
in the telephone book
writes it on a piece of paper
and leaves it near the telephone

late one evening
she picks up the telephone
and dials the number
but nobody answers

she knows she has to talk
to someone
not her son
not Mrs Briggs
not the minister
whose words at the funeral
though they brought her
to the edge of tears
were only words

she keeps a store of aspirin
in the kitchen cupboard
in case she needs them

11.

will the winter come as friend or enemy?
last winter brought his death
will this one bring hers?

when her son visits
to see how she is
and give her his news

she pretends to be well
getting on with things
as everyone must

her brother was right
when he said
we all have it to deal with

I'm all right
she says
don't worry about me

she has made dinner
as she used to do every morning
when his father was at work

mother and son sit down

to the meal he remembers having
when there were three of them

she does the washing up
while he has forty winks
as his father used to do

before he leaves
he tells her about the cottage
they are having renovated

it is twenty miles from his school
on the edge of a village
in the Shropshire countryside

they are looking forward
to moving in the spring
when the renovation is finished

if he could find a little cottage
just big enough for her
with a little garden

would she like to
sell her house
and move nearer to them?

she says it's up to him
she will leave it all to him
do whatever he says

after he has gone
she feels her spirit rise
just a little

invited by her daughter-in-law's family
to spend Christmas with them
Dorothy waits a little apprehensively
for her son to pick her up
in the car he has bought
to replace his father's

she has never spent Christmas
anywhere but in her own home
never except on holiday
slept in someone else's house
since the time she stayed
at Mary's house and wouldn't talk

she feels out of place
the odd one out
among the husband and wife
and their three married children
the only one alone
the only one who doesn't drink

you don't drink
you don't smoke
what do you do?
her son's father-in-law jokes

only speaking when she is spoken to
she is oppressed by her own silence
as much as by the voices
that are raised all around her

she asks her son to drive her home
on Boxing Day
before the midday meal
before hearing his father-in-law
announce that the bar is open
watching everyone
go out to fill their glasses
turning down their invitations
to bring something for her

it was not the Christmas
they had enjoyed
when it was just them
when Rowland would smoke a cigar
and drink a glass of sherry
before reverting
for another year
to his normal
cigarette-smoking
teetotal self

nobody tries to persuade her to stay
they have made her welcome
but it has not worked out
they can see that she is anxious to leave
so they let her go

you go back now
she tells him
before she has even
got out of the car

he comes in with her
but leaves after half an hour
to be back in time
for Boxing Day lunch
and the opening of the bar

13.

Dorothy is in her garden
listening to Neil
talking about his garden

it's just a grassy slope
he says
with a few old trees
and a stream at the bottom
I've been going every weekend
digging up the grass
stacking the turves
they've taken the roof off the house
it's more or less just four walls now
one of the walls upstairs
is wattle and daub
there's an old copper
in the kitchen
but I don't think it's worth saving

she is watching a robin
on the lilac
flitting from one branch
to another

that's your dad
she says

14.

it's up to you
she says
when her son rings
to tell her about a house
he thinks might suit her

it's in a small village
more of a hamlet really
an old semi-detached cottage
with a garden

it's been empty for a while
but not as long as theirs was
it needs some work doing
but not much

would you like to see it?
I could arrange a viewing
and pick you up next weekend
what do you think?

there's no need
she says
I'll just go by what you say
it's up to you

15.

she sometimes feels as if
she is the one who has died
as if the house is haunted
and she is the ghost

she used to say that Rowland
had one foot in this world
and one foot in the next
which was why the business failed

she thinks the same might
be true of her now
as if he has taken her with him

she still hears him sometimes
saying her name just before he died

she relies on her son
to know what is real
to do what has to be done
to keep her feet on the ground
to keep her alive

he comes to stay for a few days
during his half-term holiday
by the time he goes home again
he has found a solicitor
arranged power of attorney
and put the house up for sale

alone again after he has gone
she feels insubstantial
as if she could walk through walls

16.

when people come to see the house
she can tell those who are genuine
from those who are just nosy
her mother used to keep an eye
on people who looked as if
they might steal things
she lets them look round on their own
if they want to steal let them steal

sometimes she feels like
making a bonfire of it all

it goes on for three weeks
but it feels longer
Neil telephones to tell her
that someone has made an offer
which he thinks she should accept
she tells him again
that it's up to him
I'm past it
she says
I'm too old
though she has only just had her sixtieth birthday

she puts the telephone down
catching sight of herself

in the mirror on the coat stand
she stares at her reflection
wants to cry
wants to scream
feels like banging her head on the wall
or hanging herself from one of the coat pegs

telling herself that she has
caused enough trouble already
she turns away
goes out to the empty garage
wheels out the lawnmower
and begins cutting the grass

17.

Dorothy's one hope
when she moves into the cottage
is not that she would be happy there
she knows by the end of the first day
there is no hope of that
just that she won't cause any trouble

what is the point of living?
she thinks
what use is she to anyone?

the cottage bears no witness
to those who lived here before
many though they must have been
all she knows is
she is not welcome
they want her to go

every night while she is sleeping
they gather round her bed
watching her
wishing her ill
she never sees them
but she knows they are there

her son comes to see her
at weekends
or on his way home from work
she is glad to see him
and he is glad
to know that she is settling in

her neighbours are the man next door
who lives alone
and keeps himself to himself
and a retired couple
whose house she can see
over her garden fence

he is a retired farmer
they bring her fruit and vegetables
from their garden and greenhouse
they are kind and generous
and live in a world
far removed from hers

she dreads the approach of winter
she knows she must leave
before the first frost
the frost will kill her
if she doesn't
kill herself first

one day in autumn
when her son comes
to spend an afternoon with her
she tells him she can't go on
you'll have to send me back
she says

he is patient with her
tells her to give it more time
it's only been a few months
he says
you don't know what it's like
she says
how can I send you back?
he says
give it time
be patient
you'll get used to it
you'll be a grandmother soon
don't you want to wait for that?

she hates it
when he talks to her like this
like a teacher
you'd better go now
she says
I've had enough of you

he looks hurt
but so is she
he needs to be taught a lesson
then she thinks
but so do I
it was my fault for letting it happen

go on
she says
you need to be with your wife
not your mother
go on now
I'm all right

he goes
putting it behind him
thinking it's just a matter of time

until late one evening
her next-door neighbour telephones
to tell him his mother
is banging on the bedroom wall

18.

he lets himself in
goes upstairs
and finds her sitting on the bed
she tells him she has taken some tablets
how many?
all of them
what were they?
aspirins

at the hospital
they examine her
ask him a few questions
and go away

half an hour later a doctor comes
he says they will do
what they always do
in cases like this
pump her stomach out

she won't want to have it done again
he says

19.

I can't stand it
she says
I'll have to go back
I'll do it again
if you make me stay here

her next-door neighbour
catches sight of him
when he leaves
she needs help
he says
she can't manage on her own

assured by his wife and their friends
that it wasn't his fault
it was done with the best intentions
it just didn't work out
he puts the cottage up for sale

when she's gone back
they can put it all behind them
and forget it ever happened

it seems too good to be true
that as soon as he starts to look
he should find a house for sale
next door to the house they lived in
before Heather died

he sends for the details
but when he shows them to her
she doesn't want to look
it's up to you
she says

he leaves them with her

less than a year after she left
he takes her back
after an episode
that is best forgotten

he pulls up on the road
where he used to play
the removal van is waiting
he helps her out of the car
takes her inside

the removal men bring a chair
for her to sit on
then bring in the rest
which doesn't take long

when they have gone
he lights a cigarette
finds an ashtray
and sits down with her

she is sitting on the edge of her chair
her face is thin
lined with anxiety
I can't stay here
she says
you'll have to take me to the doctor

she still has her coat on
they walk to the doctor's
she never sees the house again
by the end of the day
she has been admitted
to a psychiatric hospital

20.

she is glad to be rid of him
the sound of his voice
grates on her
she has nothing to say to him

she recalls a saying of her mother's
you never see a young bird feed an old one

she hopes they will let her stay here
though there is nothing wrong with her
she is not mad
perhaps she should pretend to be
she remembers
banging on the bedroom wall
swallowing the tablets one by one
perhaps that will be enough

to persuade them
she remembers what it felt like
to be back in that street
sitting on a chair in an empty room
knowing that if she stayed
she would have to try
to kill herself again
she remembers the receptionist at the surgery
who has known her for years
who took one look at her and knew
don't go in the waiting room
she said
just wait here
she thinks of Rowland on the bus
coming back from hospital
standing on the platform

mad or not
they let her stay
the other patients don't look mad
there is one who cries a lot
but most of them are just quiet
she doesn't feel like crying
she is sometimes quiet
but speaks more than usual
being among strangers
she feels free
being with her son
has become burdensome
he wears her down
with his teacher's voice
his arrogance
his childishness
she thinks of St Paul

when I was a child
I thought as a child
now I am a man
I put away childish things
until that happens
she's glad to be rid of him

21.

at her first group therapy session
they tell the patients
to let their minds wander
she thinks the tablets they give them
are supposed to help with that
they tell them to think of the hospital
as a refuge and ask each of them to say
what they want to bring with them
and what they want to leave outside

when it's her turn
she says she wants
to keep her son with her
as he used to be
when he was a little lad
but not as he is now
the new one can wait outside

she remembers when they used to
go for a drive at weekends
if the weather was nice
they used to stop in a lay-by
to eat the sandwiches she made

Rowland used to say
let's find a lay-by and get stuck in
it was his catchphrase
it made them laugh
it has been a long time
she thinks
since they laughed
not since Neil left home
he lost his sense of humour
in the end
he tried to hang onto it
but she took it away
one evening he came home in tears
I can't work any more
he said
she should have put her arms round him
she should have comforted him
she should have got a job herself
but she couldn't do any of that
all she had ever been was a housewife
and a poor one at that

at the first therapy session
she has on her own
instead of talking about whether
to keep her son with her
or leave him outside
they tell her they have decided
to transfer her
to a hospital in Shropshire
where her son will be able
to visit her more often

when her son comes to see her
before she is transferred
he tells her that as well as seeing her
he is going to see the estate agent
about putting the house up for sale again
and the solicitor about legal arrangements

I just want to be left in peace
she says
just do what you have to do
and go back to your wife
you'd be better off without me

the only difference when he visits her next
is that she is in a different hospital
a ten-minute drive from where he lives

he visits her two or three times a week
to no apparent purpose
coming on his own
until the baby is born

his wife is hurt by her mother-in-law's
seeming indifference when they bring
her granddaughter with them
and sees no point in taking her again

Dorothy says to her son
she is sorry
but she can't help it
you'll just have to put up with me
she says

have a look at this
Dorothy's social worker says
pointing to a photograph
in the houses for sale pages
in the local paper
I think this might suit you
shall we go and have a look?

I should never have left it to him
Dorothy thinks
how could he be expected to know
what would suit me?
it was my fault again

the lady who shows them round
tells them she has recently lost her husband
he always loved this house
she says

what do you think?
the social worker says
when they get back into her car

what do you think?
Dorothy says

it doesn't matter what I think
it's you that will be living there
can you see yourself living there?

Dorothy says she thinks she can

24.

the soil in the garden
is like dust

not a worm
to be seen

she buries her vegetable peelings
every day

and day by day
the worms return

the social worker keeps an eye on her
more like a friend than a social worker

you need a routine to steady you
she says

Dorothy walks into town across the park
on the same days every week

on Monday she goes to the post office
to collect her pension

on Tuesday and Saturday
she goes to the market

on Thursday she goes to the library
to change her books

on Friday she walks up the road
to the supermarket

she listens to the daily service
every day on the wireless
on Sunday
she goes to chapel

the minister comes to see her
sometimes his wife comes too

you've got a nice little place here
she says

which makes Dorothy think
she must have done the right thing

25.

she doesn't need her son
she has her house
and her routine
and her impoverished garden

she doesn't need him
but when he comes
she is glad to see him

when he asks her
to go home with him
to see his daughter
she says no

when he comes with his wife
and their baby daughter
she lets them sit the baby on her lap
but not for long

you'd better take her now
she says
I'm afraid she might fall off

she is glad to see them
and glad to see them go

she has her house
and her impoverished garden
and that is enough

there are no ghosts here
unless it is the ghost of the man
who loved this house before her

26.

when she has enough put by
she buys new furniture
from Woolworths
on the high street

a drop-leaf table
a Welsh dresser
with shelves for ornaments
and cupboards for odds and ends

she has a gas fire installed
in the open fireplace
so that she can make toast
on her old toasting fork

her son buys her a fridge
which she never switches on
she puts things on it
but never in it

she has always had a pantry
to keep food in
now she avoids buying
anything that might go off

she uses powdered milk
cooks bacon and sausages
when they're fresh
and eats them cold

nothing goes to waste
when she drains vegetables
she saves the water
and drinks it

she expects to be told off
by her schoolmaster son
for her old-fashioned ways
and is thankful when she isn't

he seems to be changing
he lets her have her way now
instead of laying down the law
the way he used to do

perhaps
she thinks
he is becoming
more like his father

27.

she is a grandma now

before they are old enough to go to school
she looks after her grandchildren
first Katy
then Beccy
dropped off at her house
by her son or his wife
on their way to work

she buys jigsaws for them
which they like doing
no matter how many times
they have done them before
she plays snakes and ladders with them
they play with the dominoes
that Neil and his dad
used to play with
she keeps the toys and games
in a cupboard in the dresser
if they ask for anything
she says
go and get it
you know where it is

she keeps a cushion
embroidered with buttercups
for them to lay their heads on
when they feel sleepy
in the afternoon

buttercups
buttercups
send me to sleep
she whispers

each in her turn sits on her knee
plays on the little lawn
in the greatly enriched back garden
with its growing population
of long fat healthy worms
rides in the buggy to the supermarket
walks across the footbridge to the park
holding Grandma's hand
plays in the children's playground
kneels on the armchair
looking out of the window
for Mummy or Daddy
when it's time for them to go home

when they have gone
she tidies up
and makes her tea

she walks one morning on planks
laid across the flooded road
on her way to the market

a man in wellington boots
offers a helping hand
and smiles encouragement

perhaps the little old lady
with her white hair
and her shopping basket

toddling and tottering
across the flooded road
past the furious river

looks to him not quite real
more like a picture in a storybook
Mrs Tiggywinkle perhaps

after so many years of serving her
the traders in the market hall
know what she wants without asking

too short-sighted to find the right change
she gives them her purse instead
and they help themselves

the market is quiet this morning
some of the stalls are closed
because of the floods

they ask her how she got there
she says the footbridge was closed
so she had to use the road bridge instead

how did you manage that?
she tells them about the planks
across the flooded road

didn't you see the signs?
she points to her glasses
you're very brave!

sometimes she feels
as if she has lived here
all her life

everything that went before
the farm the shop the village
as if it had never been

she feels safe here
even when the river overflows
and she has to walk on planks

but every morning she wakes
from dreams of the past
that never leave her

dreams of things
too vividly remembered
not to be real

her daily routine is all
that saves her
from drowning

when her grandchildren are older
she spends Saturday mornings
cooking dinner for five

there is always a choice
roast chicken shepherd's pie
sprouts cabbage cauliflower carrots swede
mashed potatoes roast potatoes
gravy Yorkshire pudding
rice pudding apple pie jelly

she doesn't have a table big enough
for them all to sit round
the children sit on the floor
the grown-ups balance their plates
on kitchen stools
or their knees

after they have eaten
the children ask if they can play
with the things they played with
when they were little
the older they get
the more they seem to enjoy them
their parents talk
she washes up
refusing all offers of help
her husband and son
never washed up
she wouldn't let them

she goes to church now
church and chapel merged
when the Methodist congregation
dwindled almost to nothing
it's the vicar who comes to see her now

when her son came to see the house
before she bought it
he thought it might not be suitable
a busy road
people walking past
outside the window
only a little front garden
between the house and the road

that's what I want
she said
you don't understand
I want to see movement outside

she meant not like the house
he had chosen for her
where she was so lonely
it nearly drove her mad

30.

he makes her a bird table
for her birthday
she is eighty-three

she remembers the matchbox holder
he made at school
in woodwork lessons

the woodwork teacher's name
she remembers
was Hector Lamb

Mr Lamb
Hector
was his nickname

Rowland fastened the matchbox holder
to the wall beside the cooker
it must still be there

so much has been lost
Rowland's drawing of Lake Garda
went missing

she thinks one of the people
who came to see the house
must have stolen it

she had been confused
groping in the dark
losing her way

so much money wasted
moving house
buying and selling

but she has a house again now
a few thousand pounds in the bank
and a widow's pension to live on

enough for her wants
more than enough
she is safe now

the bird table has a proper roof
he has made a good job of it
as good as the matchbox holder

he digs a hole for the post
she holds it in place
while he pours concrete into the hole

she threads monkey nuts on a string
and hangs them up
for the tits to peck at

where have all the birds gone?
she asks him
I never hear them now

the birds are still there
it's just that you can't hear them
you can't always hear me

that's because you mutter
she says
you should speak up

31.

her eyes have been troubling her
more than her ears
she goes to the optician
the optician refers her to the hospital

they say I've got glaucoma
she tells her son
I've got to have an operation
they say it's urgent

the glaucoma is more advanced
in her right eye
too late to save that
just a chance they might save the other

the operation was painful
the surgeon was late
the anaesthetic was wearing off
before he had finished

sorry about that
he said when it was over
you're a brave little lady
well done

eye drops every night
and regular appointments
at the eye clinic
are part of her routine now

part of her son's too
helping with the eye drops
driving her to the clinic
waiting with her in the queue

if she has to wait
more than a few minutes
she grows impatient
and threatens to leave

he wishes he could give her
something to play with
as he does with his children
when they grow fractious

all he can do for
his mother
is try to set her
a good example

I can't put up with this much longer
she says
he pats her hand
it won't be long now

time passes
the reversal of roles
between mother and son
feels strange

32.

when a cataract is diagnosed
at the eye clinic
they tell her she can have an operation
to have it removed
and put her on a waiting list

the morning after the operation
when she wakes up
and opens her eyes
she can see nothing
the operation must have failed

it works
for most people
but not for her
nothing ever does
she should have known

raising her hand
to her eyes
she touches the blindfold
she has forgotten
she is wearing

you must keep it on
all night
the doctor said
take it off
in the morning

the elastic
catches on her hair
as she pulls the blindfold
over her head
and looks round

but nothing has changed
everything looks the same
it has all been
a waste of time
all that for nothing

she sits on the edge of the bed
wishing she hadn't let them
persuade her to do it
what was the point
at her age?

she looks at the clock
quarter past seven
the early morning sun
faint through the curtains
everything looks dull
and drab and pale

until the sun parts the curtains
leans in
puffs out its cheeks
and blows
and a magician runs in
pulling coloured scarves
from his sleeves

and the clothes she folded
before she went to bed
unfold in a whirlpool of colour
and the room spins round
in a Busby Berkeley
technicolor dance routine
and she can see
better than ever before
without her glasses on

it's a miracle!
a miracle!

thank you!
she says
thank you!
thank you!
thank you!

33.

though she still has
almost no sight in one eye
the other is as good as new
so good that for the first time
in more than seventy years
she doesn't have to wear glasses

but she still reaches for them
when she's getting dressed
and her hand still tries
to push them up her nose

even when there is nothing there
to slide down it

she can see the coins in her purse now
but she has forgotten which is which
so she goes on paying at the market
in the way they have all got used to
if they think she looks different in some way
they can't work out what has changed

she sees less of her grandchildren now
the eldest is at university already
the youngest will follow soon enough
Katy has gone to Durham like her mother
which reminds her of the day
Rowland fell on the pavement

that reminds her of the day in June
when they drove to Cambridge
to bring Neil home on his last day
it was the only time they went
she had never seen Rowland look happier
than he did that day at Neil's college

he would have been sorry to see
their son's marriage come to an end
at least his death has spared him that
she is sorry too
but somehow when it happened
it seemed as if it had to

early on the morning of Christmas Day
for the last three Christmases
he had left his wife and children

at her parents' home
and driven for an hour to spend
half an hour with her before driving back

after the third Christmas Day
when he told her
he had decided
to leave his wife
she was sad
but not surprised

on the fourth Christmas Day
in the morning sunshine
she walks along the riverbank
to have Christmas dinner with him
he meets her halfway and they walk together
to his flat on the other side of the river

it is the first time since Rowland died
that she has not been alone at Christmas
except when she was alone with her son
in a house full of people
did she take him from them?
she puts the thought from her mind

the grandchildren who once fell asleep
on a cushion embroidered with buttercups
while she whispered a magic spell
bring their boyfriends to meet her now
they still remember the cushion
and show it to the bemused young men

when Beccy comes one Christmas
the youngest and littlest
the one she spent most time with
the one who was most like her
when she said
I won't talk Mary

she still sees the little girl
in the young woman
and feels sorry for the boyfriend
who has been dragged along
and would rather be somewhere else
who can blame him?

standing up to see them out
she feels her head spin
as if something has come loose
and falls back again
oh Grandma!
what's wrong?

I'm all right
are you sure Grandma?
I'm sure
you go now
go on
I'm all right

Everyone will be so happy

his daughter phoned him
Grandma seems confused
she said
we've just left her
I'm worried but I didn't know what to do
she said she was all right
I think you should go and see her

she was slumped on the settee
the left side of her face distorted
he rang for an ambulance
the ambulance men came in
looked at her
told her she'd had a stroke
she gave them half a smile
they tidied her up
and put her in the ambulance

the delirium started
on the second day
he went to see her
but she didn't know who he was
she kept talking about water
when he tried to calm her
she fought him off

on the third day
when he found her sleeping
he put his head close to hers
and told her he loved her
thinking she would die

2.

her feet are wet
she needs to change her slippers

water is trickling splashing
all around her

her clothes are soaked
the water is rising

drip drip drip
her bed is floating

her slippers are in the water
she can't reach them

every time she tries
someone stops her

she is lying on the floor
a man is looking down at her

he shouts at her
what are you doing down there?

he picks her up
and drops her

water laps round
she closes her eyes

thinking she must be drowning
drowning

3.

the right side of her face
is one livid purple bruise

her son is shocked when he sees her
he asks the nurse how it happened

she fell out of bed in the night
the ward orderly found her on the floor

she has been delirious for two days
he says

it often happens with a stroke
she says

you mean because of the medication?
but the nurse has gone

the next day his mother has gone
and he fears the worst

but it is not that
they have moved her to the stroke ward

this is a general ward
the nurse explains

the stroke ward was full before
we've found a bed for her now

4.

cared for by the ambulance men
given nightmares on the general ward
recovering on the stroke ward
she becomes a favourite with the nurses
when she begins physiotherapy

she makes them laugh
when she tells them
about doing her exercises in the bath

I can put my toes in my mouth
I bet you can't

Dorothy
they say
you're a hoot!

her son brings her flowers from her garden
on her birthday
he has gathered them that morning

early daffodils
pussy willow
jasmine

oh what lovely flowers!
the nurses say

my son brought them
it's my birthday
I'm eighty-nine

eighty-nine!
and you can still get your toes in your mouth!

5.

six weeks after the stroke
they send her home
with a collection of implements
to help her walk
sit
stand up
wash herself
pick things up
and go to the toilet

the bruise on her face
is hardly noticeable now
her son has begun a correspondence
with the hospital
which goes on for weeks
and ends only when he tires

of the hospital managers'
jargon-ridden obfuscation
and throws in the towel

she is glad to be home again
but soon finds that she can't do
all the things she used to do
she can't lift her arms high enough
to hang her washing on the line
she can't walk across the park
to the market
or the library
or the hairdresser's

I thought I could carry on like I did before
she says
but I can't

after a few weeks
he suggests
buying a house
where they can live together

she says she doesn't want
to be a burden to him

he says she won't be

6.

in the summer
not long after his fifty-ninth birthday

he meets the removal men
at her house
which has been sold
for more than the asking price
after a Saturday morning
bidding war
unlike his flat
which has yet to find a buyer

after a final look round the house
which has been her home
for thirty years
loved by her
as much as by anyone
but left with no regrets
they follow the removal van
to their new house

it is an old house
a tall thin town house
in a narrow passage
in the medieval town centre
with a vaulted cellar
and rooms on three floors
one to share
one for her
one for him

it's so quiet
he says
after the removal men have gone
you wouldn't think you were
in the middle of the town

she does not reply

he remembers then
that the busy road
was what she liked about her old house

has this been another mistake?

if it has
it's too late
to do anything about it

she goes to bed early
he makes sure
before he leaves her
that she knows
where everything is

he tells her to be careful
going downstairs in the morning
better wait till I get up
he says
until you get used to it

she wants to be rid of him
to be on her own
he kisses her goodnight

in the morning
she waits for him
before she goes downstairs

while he's out at work
she does her chores

she washes up
after breakfast

goes upstairs
to do her housework

carries her Ewbank down
to sweep downstairs

the same tasks are carried out
on the same day

in the same order
every week

dusting and polishing
sweeping the carpet

cleaning the toilet
cleaning the bath

washing her underwear
in the bathroom sink

a life-saving
daily routine

on her floor
on the ground floor

upstairs and downstairs
everywhere except the master's chamber

which he says
she must leave to him

always the same
giving his orders

while he is out at work
curiosity gets the better of her

she climbs to the top floor
opens his door and looks inside

on the way back down
she misses the bottom step

falls headlong
on the landing

telltale bruising
forces a confession

he tells her off
as if she's a child

hurt and aggrieved
she shuts herself away

behind closed doors
inside her room

behind closed mouth
inside her head

until one day
by tacit consent

the incident is forgotten
and life goes on as before

he takes her to the library
which is just down the road

he takes her to the hairdresser's
which is even nearer

the librarians and the hairdresser
are pleased to see her again

when she feels ready
they walk together to the market

where both are known
though not as mother and son

she is greeted with surprise
and given a warm welcome

by people who have known
her for more than twenty years

and taken change from her purse
for the last ten

is she your mother?
we thought she'd passed away

the walk home
is all uphill

he takes her hand
she pulls it back

don't fight me
he says

he takes her hand again
and this time

reluctantly
she lets him hold it

8.

Rajpal is here
her son says
he's come to say hello

she has seen photographs of him
taken when her son
met him in India
and made friends with him

a tall dark handsome man
wearing a bright yellow turban
walks into her room

hello Mom
he says
kneeling in front of her
as if he were
one of the three kings
who travelled from the east
following a star
which they expected
to lead them to a baby
but which has brought them instead
to an old woman

mistakes happen
signs are misinterpreted
a wise man
knows how easily
an old woman
can be mistaken
for a baby

lacking precious gifts
he touches her feet
and offers her instead
tidings of great joy

next year
Neil says
will be our sesquicentenary

between us
we will have lived
for a hundred and fifty years
Mum will be ninety in February
and I will be sixty in May

this is wonderful!
Rajpal exclaims
you must come to India
to celebrate with us

Dorothy smiles
the smile of one who hears
but does not comprehend

her son explains
that she has been invited
to spend her birthday
next year
with Rajpal
in India

would you like that?

I would
she says
looking up at Rajpal
very much

Rajpal's eyes open wide
he grasps her hands in his
you must come!
he says
everyone will be so happy!

India

I thought I'd died and gone to heaven is one of those things that people say but don't really mean. Not literally. But in Dorothy's case, when she woke up on the day she was going to fly to India, she really did think she had died and gone to heaven. What else could have caused her to wake up feeling happy? The leaden weight that was always there had gone as if it had been taken from her during the night by some kind spirit, some angel. The angel of death must have taken pity on her at last and carried her up to heaven. The last time she remembered waking up happy was when she was seven and woke up remembering that today was the day she was going to stay with John and Milly. Was her life over? Was she in heaven now with Heather and Rowland? She stopped thinking. Too much thinking might chase the happiness away. She was happy. Happy and awake! She was more than happy, she was joyful. She told her son about it when she went downstairs. I woke up this morning with a feeling of joy. That's the only word I can find for it. Joy.

A giant horse gallops through the open gate of heaven. The rider reaches down as he passes and gathers her up. She sleeps curled up on the palm of his open hand. In the night she sees her husband and their daughter dancing on the roof of their mansion. In the morning her son tells a woman in a green sari that his mother is going to India for her ninetieth birthday. The woman puts her hands together, leans towards her and smiles. I hope you will wear Indian attire on your birthday.

Amritsar is outside the car window. Dorothy's son looks at her looking at Amritsar. Shops spilling out over the pavements. Stalls piled high with vegetables. Cars, trucks, buses, bicycles, carts, scooters, rickshaws. Women with babies in their arms begging among the traffic. Men in turbans riding motorcycles with two, three, four passengers. Cows. Her face gives nothing away. Has this been another mistake? Taking an old woman who has never been out of England to spend her ninetieth birthday in India. One more thing to regret? Her eyes are open wide. Only one of them can see, but it can see well enough now. What does she see? What is she thinking? Finally, he asks her. She answers, her eyes wide with wonder. I can't believe I'm here.

From Amritsar to Chandigarh is a four-hour drive with little to see except green fields. Canals catch the sun like filaments of silver. Women with shawls over their heads sit beside dungheaps in farmyards. Slender brown hands pat and slap and shape and turn and toss. Patchwork patterns in shades of brown dry in the sun. Every few miles a brick kiln's tall brick chimney pierces the sky. At the roadside, men with loose turbans draw long wooden rakes over vats of gold, making sweet brown jaggery out of sugar cane and sunshine. A man in a bright blue turban, tied Patiala-style, drives an old English woman and her son in a little white car across the plains of Punjab from Amritsar to Chandigarh. The two men talk sporadically to each other, point things out to her. She looks out of the window, enunciates a thought. I feel as if I've been here before. He feels her hand on his arm. Thank you. He looks at her and sees that she is crying.

After ninety years, five hours sleep more or less makes little difference. Dorothy falls into step with the Indian sun as easily as if he were an old and trusted friend. After all, she has been here before, though until now she didn't know. Today is her birthday, but the celebration is to come later. There is a small park a hundred yards down the road from Rajpal's house. Rajpal and his wife have gone shopping in the little white car. Dorothy and her son walk to the park. He offers his hand. I've got my stick. I'm all right. A footpath runs all the way round the park, with flower beds alongside it. An English park in India. Flowers of an English June in an Indian February. Marigolds, snapdragons, petunias, pansies, nasturtiums, geraniums, roses. The white-haired old lady and her white-haired son walk hand in hand all the way round the park, stopping every few yards to look at the flowers. Back where they started, they sit down on a bench in the shade of an Indian tree, the Indian sun lapping at their feet. On the other side of the park, two men in turbans sit cross-legged on the grass, playing cards. Behind the men, two women in shawls sit on a bench. A baby crawls on the grass. Dorothy's son asks her if she is glad she said yes when Rajpal invited her to spend her birthday in India. She tells him she is glad now, but confesses that she didn't really mean it. I only said yes because I thought I'd be dead by now.

This one is different. A changeling. She has been here before. Bemused, beatific, in India on her ninetieth birthday, Dorothy sits on a divan, a pauper in a palace. Someone brings in the birthday cake. Someone puts a knife in her hand. Her son puts her hand in his and, guided by him, she cuts the first slice. Everyone claps and queues for cake. One by one, two by two, the guests approach the divan, stoop to touch her feet and lay their gifts on the table in front of her.

All but one bring roses. The last gift has to be unwrapped by her son. He gasps when he sees what it is, then holds it in front of her. Turning her head this way and that until her good eye has it clearly in view, she sees herself. Her portrait. Rajpal, whose gift it is, introduces the artist, a handsome young man dressed all in white. She smiles. Very handsome. The artist introduces his wife, a beautiful young woman dressed all in pink. Very beautiful. She thinks they look like the pink and white figures made of icing on a wedding cake.

If there are rainbows in India, they are draped now over the shoulders of beautiful, smiling, charming, rose-bearing Indian girls. Ninety-year-old Dorothy sees in the colours of their Indian attire the colours of the sky at sunrise and sunset, colours without number or name, such as were never seen on Rowland's wan palette. He took his colours from the hills and fields of England. What else could he do? The white-haired changeling sees colours now that, had she not been stolen from her crib by jealous fairies, would have been her birthright. Dressed in Indian attire, the girl she once was could have been as beautiful as those who surround her now, floating like rose petals on water.

A grey-haired lady comes to speak to her. Her son makes room on the divan for her to sit. She takes something out of a small box. Dorothy looks but sees nothing. Even with her good eye, it is invisible. The lady places her invisible gift on Dorothy's hand. As she looks, a little glass elephant appears. It has arms and a trunk and a hat and stands upright on a glass plinth. She looks to her son for help. He tells her that it is an Indian god called Ganesh. He says the lady has given it to her because Ganesh is the god of new beginnings.

She says he will help her in the new beginning that she is making now on her ninetieth birthday. Smiling, the grey-haired lady nods and speaks again. Her son explains that she is asking her to share with them some of the wisdom that she has acquired in her ninety years of life. Dorothy feels as she always did at school when a teacher asked her a question. She always knew the answer but never dared to say it in case she was wrong. She was always right. The lady waits patiently. What has she learned that young people can learn from her? Dorothy thinks for a long time before she gives her answer. I don't think I've learned anything.

Refusing her son's hand, on what Dorothy would be happy to make her morning walk on every day of what remains of her life, she sees what looks like last night's Indian attire hanging out to dry on washing lines and hedges and windowsills. Even the washing looks nicer here. They stop at the park and sit on the bench that she would like to be theirs forever, looking across the dew-soaked grass at flowers that seem to grow in another time as well as another place. Everything is nicer here. An invisible veil hangs from the sky. The sky is the sea and they are under it. Where does it come from, this happiness, this joy? She opens her arms wide. I want to scoop it all up and take it home with me.

Being very small and very old, very happy and very white, Dorothy is the cynosure of Indian eyes. But she does not notice it. Walking with her son in the Rose Garden, she does not notice the young woman who walks behind them. Her hand still reaches for the glasses that she no longer wears. Her good eye sees only what her head turns to look at. Everyman, I will go with thee, in thy most need to go by thy side. So said Knowledge in the old play. Dorothy's son plays that part now. Only between her lying down and rising is he not by her side. She goes to bed early. When he judges her to be in bed, he goes to her room to say goodnight. She turns her head and looks up at him. Her toothless smile (for her teeth are in a glass on the bedside table) gives her the face of a baby and makes him feel as if in the passage of time they have changed places. Walking together in the Rose Garden, neither of them notices the young woman who walks behind them. Only when Rajpal joins them does she step forward and make her request. She wishes to be allowed to walk with her, Rajpal explains. She is a student at the university and has been wanting to speak, but she is shy and her English is not very good. Dorothy would take her home with her if she could and is very happy to have a beautiful Indian girl walk by her side instead of her son. An old white rose and a new yellow rose walk hand in hand among all the June roses that are blooming in the February Rose Garden. When they reach the car park and say their goodbyes, the yellow rose stands and waves and waves and waves as the little white car drives away, and in the car the tears flow freely from Dorothy's eyes.

The man who cycles around the streets pulling a cart full of vegetables, calling his wares in a sing-song voice, stopping to serve the women who come out of their houses to buy onions, potatoes, carrots, turnips, tomatoes, which he weighs for them on a pair of old-fashioned scales; the man who cycles around the streets selling orange juice from a cart full of oranges which he squeezes into whatever vessels the women who come out from their houses give him to hold; the tailor with a tape measure round his neck, at whose long counter she sits on the chair he brings for her, facing shelves laden with rolls of fabric which he summons young men to pull down and roll out for her inspection, while a boy offers her water in a glass made of steel and the young men, like sorcerers' apprentices, pull down more and more rolls of fabric until the counter is awash with waves of colour, until she makes her choice and the tailor whisks the tape measure from his neck and asks her to stand while he takes her measurements, reading them out for another young man to write down, before turning to her son and asking him if he would like to be measured for a suit; the man sitting at an old Singer sewing machine in the market who smiles at her and beckons her to sit on a chair beside him and rest for a while; the armed policemen lounging outside the hotel, who jump to their feet and hold the door open for her; the man sitting in a barber's chair on the pavement; the handcarts; the horse carts; all make her feel at home. This is how things used to be.

One day, Rajpal takes Dorothy and her son to his village. Many years ago, he says, one of the Sikh gurus visited his ancestor here. Today we are twice blessed. He shows them the house where he grew up, an old house with a verandah and a spacious courtyard. He points to an upper floor where, he says, his mother and the other women lived. His relatives come out to greet them, among them a young woman who asks to be allowed to show them round. Walking beside Dorothy, speaking English, she leads them along the quiet lanes and narrow passageways of the ancestral village. She takes Dorothy's arm as they climb some steps. When they reach the top of the steps, she hears sobbing. Though not tall herself, she must bend down to see the old lady by her side. Seeing her take out a handkerchief to dry her eyes, she turns anxiously to the lady's son, wondering what she has done to

Something unusual is going to happen. Three armchairs have been put out in a dusty square beside a high brick wall on the edge of the village. Some boys lean against the wall, watching. A little white car approaches and stops near the armchairs. The driver, a tall Indian man wearing a pink turban tied Patiala-style, leads his passengers to the armchairs. The boys watch as one of them, an old lady, drops into one of the armchairs and disappears. One of the others, a white man, holds her hands and pulls her up while the man in the pink turban slips a cushion under her. The white man lowers her onto it. The top of Dorothy's head can now be seen. A door opens in the wall. Five bearded men and two women come out. The boys know what is going to happen now and sit down to watch. The men wear red shirts, yellow trousers, white sandals and yellow turbans tied Peshawari-style. The women are barefoot, with many bangles on their arms and shawls draped loosely over their heads. All but one of the men have drums slung over their shoulders, the other has a black pipe in his hand and a red windbag under his arm. The women, who are also men, finger their shawls and push back their long black hair. Rajpal jumps up to greet them, exchanges a few words, then returns to his chair. Moments later, the drummers drum up four kinds of thunder, the piper pipes a high wind, the women link arms in a whirlwind of dust and, at the still centre of the storm, Dorothy sits and watches. The storm blows itself out, leaving only an irregular tapping in its wake, like rain. In the lull, one of the women who are also men dances coyly towards the man in the pink turban and, reaching her arm towards him without breaking step, makes the five-hundred-rupee note that he is holding above his head disappear. A clap of thunder, a blast of wind, a barefoot tornado runs after a blown-away shawl and Dorothy sits at the heart of another storm until it subsides again. Her son gives her a five-hundred-rupee note to hold above her head. One of the dancers dances towards her, reaches out, takes the note and circles it three times around Dorothy's head, before dancing gracefully away again. He is blessing her, Rajpal whispers in Neil's ear. He is blessing you, Neil whispers in his mother's ear. Another storm breaks and, with it, Dorothy's tears. The storm passes. The musicians and dancers line up for a photograph with Dorothy. In black boots, grey skirt, white jumper and pink cardigan, with a walking stick in her hand and no glasses to push up her nose, surrounded on all sides by barefoot dancers and yellow-crested musicians, she looks joyfully at the camera. There is no other word for it. Joy.

How beautiful she is

it's better there than it is here
Dorothy says
can't we go back?

the snow in the courtyard
outside her window
is turning to slush

it's your birthday next
she says
where shall we go?

I don't mind
he says
where do you want to go?

I don't mind
she says
so long as we can fly there

in that case
he says
let's go to France

2.

every summer
and twice at Christmas
in the eight years
she has left to live
they fly to France

Rajpal asks them
when they will
come back to India
they promise to come back
when she is a hundred

there is nothing special
to remember
about her birthdays
in midwinter
in England

nothing to compare
with her birthday
when she was ninety
in midwinter summer
in India

nothing to compare
with her son's birthday
when he was sixty
in spring
in France

nothing to compare
with all the holidays
in France
in all the years
they spend together now

all the new memories
that drive out
the old ones
begin and end
in the sky

this has been
the best part of my life
she says one evening
when her son tucks her in
and kisses her goodnight

3.

on holiday
one autumn
in a village
in the south
of France
they drive
to nearby
St Tropez
the road
is busy
too busy
turning back

they see
a sign
to the beach
the sand
at the end
of a narrow road
is ankle-deep
the sea
deepest blue
just fancy!
our Dot
on the Mediterranean!
did you see
anybody famous?
no
it was
just us

4.

another time
on holiday
in Burgundy
they visit
the medieval town
of Beaune
and the famous
Hospices de Beaune
once an almshouse
where the aged
and infirm
were cared for

in the time
of Philip the Good
the good people
on duty today
at the museum
taking pity
on the aged lady
tell her son
that his mother
may ignore
the signs
that forbid
sitting on
the ancient
wooden furniture
everyone is so kind
she says
sitting down
on a bench
polished to
a chestnut shine
by centuries
of aged and infirm
Burgundian limbs
her son stands
beside her
you'd better not
sit there
too long
he says
or they'll think
you're one of
the original
inhabitants

5.

the habits of her lifetime
are given up
one by one
always
but not wholly
with regret

she misses housework
and keeps her old Ewbank
in case it is ever needed
but looks forward
to the days when Daniela
comes to clean

the young Bulgarian woman
and the old English woman
communicate poorly in words
but very well by other means
she sends Daniela on secret errands
in May and December
to buy birthday presents
and Christmas presents
for her son
she goes shopping with him
to buy presents for Daniela

she misses walking
but soon gets used to the wheelchair
that her son buys for her
so that their Saturday morning

walk to the market can continue
he does the walking
she directs him
from stall to stall
and tells him what to buy

she misses browsing in the library
walking from shelf to shelf
to choose her books
but soon finds that letting her son
bring a selection for her to choose from
in the comfort of her wheelchair
is nearly as good

she misses being able to hear
what people are saying
but after a failed experiment
with a hearing aid
decides to put up with it

whenever anyone asks her
how she is
she invariably replies
not so bad
considering old age and poverty

6.

when Dorothy wakes up
on the first Christmas Day
in their shared home
she finds a Christmas stocking
at the foot of her bed

she is disappointed
a year later
to find that Father Christmas
has forgotten her

she enjoys the day anyway
just as she enjoys each
of the Christmas Days
that are still to come

the Christmas Day routine
is always the same

after breakfast
the opening of presents
a gift voucher
and a book token
for him
for her
whatever she has asked for

after the opening of presents
a walk in the quiet streets
pale wintry sky
pale wintry sun
early blossom
on the cherry tree
in the churchyard

after a walk
Christmas dinner
a turkey is too big for two
chicken is what they used to have at Christmas
now she asks for shepherd's pie

he calls it festive shepherd's pie
after the shepherds
who watched their flocks by night
to distinguish it from the shepherd's pie
they have for the rest of the year

after Christmas dinner
he turns on the wireless
as she still calls it
for the traditional
Festival of Nine Lessons and Carols
from King's College Cambridge

after that
Christmas Day
is just like any other day

every Christmas is the same
every Christmas Day
helps to make up
for the forty Christmas Days
she spent alone

7.

in the last decade
of his mother's life
her son is witness
to a slow transfiguration

riding in a rickshaw
at the university in Amritsar

they were flagged down
by two young women

sir they said
is she your mother?
we just want to say
how beautiful she is

seeing her in her wheelchair
at home in England
people turn to look
as she goes by

being English
they don't say
how beautiful she is
they just look and smile

in any village in France
in any church
on any wall or niche
she might have seen

a portrait or a statue
of the blessed Dorothy
that she has now become
with a halo of white hair

she might have remembered
Rowland after his death agony
emerging from his chrysalis of age
to be young again

she does not dwell much on death
but sometimes tells her son
how nice it would be to go to sleep
and not wake up in the morning

until that happens
her skin pale as parchment
shines as if lit from within
by a single candle

8.

one evening
when Dorothy is sitting alone in her room
thinking of going to bed
a girl in a green dress
comes in

Dorothy looks at the girl
the girl looks at Dorothy
then turns
and goes out

Dorothy is not afraid
when the girl in green
comes back on other nights
as she sometimes does

nor is she afraid
only surprised
when Rowland comes in
what are you doing here?

she says
he says nothing
goes out
and does not return

9.

one morning
Dorothy's son
hears her calling
Neil
Neil
he gets out of bed
puts on his dressing gown
goes down to her bedroom
finds the bed empty
Neil
Neil
following her voice
he finds her
on the other side of the bed
lying on the floor

I've been calling for ages
she says
but you didn't hear

he helps her up
she isn't hurt
or even much distressed
now that he has found her

sitting with her later
in her room
he sees the brass bell
between the two brass candlesticks
on her mantelpiece

he moves it to her bedside table
where she can reach it
and tells her to ring it
if she needs him in the night

loud and imperious
as a fireman's bell
it drags him often
from the depths of sleep

he imagines himself
sliding down a fireman's pole
to her bedside

sometimes when it rings
in the middle of the night
he wishes he had left it where it was

until he remembers finding her
lying helpless on the floor
her cries for help unheard

a memory that endures
like the memory
of her lonely Christmases
a constant rebuke

10.

when the things she can't do
outnumber the things she can
she begins to lose heart
what's the point in living?
she says
send for the doctor
and tell him to finish me off

11.

one by one
her granddaughters
bring great-grandchildren to meet her
four altogether
in as many years

she tells her son
it's nice to see the babies
but she agrees
with the doctor
who delivered him

all babies are the same
he used to say
they all look like rabbits
when they're born

he pictures a midwife
holding a newborn baby

by the ankles
its blood-streaked body
looking like a skinned rabbit
on a butcher's hook

when the babies
turn into toddlers
and start to walk and talk
she gets out the jigsaws
and the tin of dominoes
that their mothers used to play with
she still has the cushion
they laid their heads on
while she sang
buttercups
buttercups
send me to sleep
and it always did
she tells them

but when the children
start to run about
and make a noise
her son and her granddaughter
can see that she has had enough

Great-Grandma is feeling tired
they say
and send them downstairs
to play with their father

12.

have I made another mistake?
her son asks himself
when they move out of their town house
to a house in the country

how would you feel about moving
to a bungalow?
he said

every time I go out
I'm worried I'll come back
and find you at the bottom of the stairs
with a broken leg
or worse

it's up to you
she said
you know better than me
I'll do whatever you say

he rents a bungalow
on a quiet road
on the edge of a farm
in the middle of nowhere
with a garden

all they can see
from the house
is fields and sky
with kites

and buzzards
circling overhead

it's too vast
she says
looking out of the window

it reminds her
of the house he chose for her
then left her in on her own

you're not on your own now
he says
but that makes no difference
the memory
he thought had gone away
has come back
the happy memories
that came later
displaced

while he works in the garden
that was meant to bring her joy
she sits indoors
with her head in her hands
as if she is sitting
at someone's grave

13.

one evening
when they are sitting quietly together
she breaks the silence
and starts to talk

I feel as if I've been cheated
she says
all my life
I never loved your father
I turned him down
when he asked me to marry him
I told him I didn't love him
he went straight to my mother
and told her what I'd said
she said leave it to me
I just thought
do what you like
he was a good man
that's what my brother said
when he came
the day your father died
the first thing he said was
we've all had it to deal with
there was no sentiment with him
any more than there was
with any of them
I was cruel to your dad
I made his life a misery
we should never
have got married

he would have been
better off without me
it was the same for him
as it was for me
it was the same for everyone
he should have gone
to grammar school
but his parents wanted him
out working
earning money
we've taken care of you
all these years
think how much it's cost us
it's time you paid us back
that was how people looked at it
in those days
if it had been now
he would have gone to university
like you
perhaps I would too
like your daughters
I was reading before you were
so was Heather
I thought you would never start
then one day
Heather came to me in the kitchen
she said look at him
she took me with her
and pointed to you
sitting on the floor
reading the paper
it was comical really
but that was it

all of a sudden
you were reading

she fell silent
for a moment
then spoke again

I just think it was so sad
that Heather died when she did
just when she was starting
to become a woman

it was the first time
she had spoken about her
since she died
she started to cry
he went to sit next to her
and put his arm round her
this time she didn't push him away
but went on crying
and he started to cry
and they cried together

14.

sometimes
when he is working in the garden
he looks up and sees her
at the window
watching him
she smiles
he waves to her

she waves back

they seem
both far apart
and very close

15.

he notices how thin she is getting
people will think I'm starving you
he says

I'm all right
she says
it's chewing I can't manage
and swallowing

the food just goes
round and round

she slips in the bath
and he has to help her out
which is when he sees
that she is all
skin and bone

he thinks she should see a doctor
but first she sees a nurse

everything hurts
she tells her
even when I'm sitting down

while the nurse listens
to her chest
Dorothy looks down

where have they gone?
she says
as if she has only just
noticed their absence

the nurse laughs
there is nothing
she can do
about the missing breasts
but she recommends
an inflatable cushion
for sitting on

it helps a little
but she is still
uncomfortable
and unhappy

when she complains
about pains in her hip
he persuades the doctor
to make a home visit

two days later
she is admitted
to hospital
for tests

16.

an X-ray reveals
a fracture of the hip
which happened a long time ago

neither Dorothy nor her son
can remember when it might have happened

her difficulty in swallowing
is of more concern
especially as she is
finding it hard to speak
as well as swallow

the nurses feed her
on bread and milk
while a drip provides
the sustenance needed
to keep her alive

one day
when the consultant is doing his rounds
she overcomes
her difficulty in speaking
enough to say that
she wants to go home
and be allowed to die

the next time her son visits
the consultant takes him on one side
tells him what his mother said
and asks him what he thinks

his first thought is
of all the times
she has told him
to fetch a doctor
and tell him to finish her off

he hears her
saying how wonderful it would be
to go to sleep
and not wake up

he pictures her face
as she says it

she's old enough
to know her own mind
he says

when he goes to sit with his mother
she tries to tell him something
he makes out a few words
doctor
home
rejuvenate

I think you mean
resuscitate
he says
rejuvenate might be
too much to ask for

what's tickled you Dorothy?
a nurse asks when she sees them laughing

a hospital bed is installed

in their house
her son is shown
how to operate it
the next time he visits
he tells her about it
all they have to do now
he says
is find enough nurses to look after you
it takes two to turn you
he explains
and they have to be there
all the time

which is why
it takes them a long time
to find enough nurses
and in the end
proves impossible

he has to tell her
she won't be going home after all
instead she will be going
to a cottage hospital
where she will be well looked after
and he will be able to see her
whenever he likes

the nurses will look after you
better than I could
he says

she nods and smiles
and mouths
thank you

17.

mouthing
and writing in the air
are the only forms of communication
she has left

when he sees her writing in the air
he is reminded of the postcards
she used to send from France

he always wrote the address
but she was determined
to write the message herself

what did it matter
if what she wrote was illegible
so long as the postman
could read the address
and her friends could see
that she was on holiday
in France

only once
is he unable
to understand
what she is trying to say
she writes a long sentence
in the air
too many words
to be mouthed
she gives up

in the end
lets her hand fall
and smiles sadly

she mouths
I love you

I love you
he says
and holds
her bony shoulder
and kisses
her pale forehead

he spends every day
and some nights
at her bedside
wondering sometimes
what it was
she was trying to say

one morning
when he goes to see her
he finds that her face
has changed overnight
there are deep hollows
where her cheeks once were

even then
relieved of pain
by whatever means
the nurses can use
she opens her eyes sometimes
and sees him
sitting beside her
and a smile
illuminates her face